DERBYSHIRE AT WAR
1939–45

Dedication

Dedicated to all the people of Derbyshire who gave so much in the Second World War to the military fronts and on the Home Front in their determination that Hitler should not win the war; and especially to those Derbyshire people who made the supreme sacrifice so that fascism would not win and Britain could remain a free country.

YOUR TOWNS & CITIES IN WORLD WAR TWO

DERBYSHIRE AT WAR
1939–45

GLYNIS COOPER

Pen & Sword
MILITARY

First published in Great Britain in 2019 by
Pen & Sword Military
An imprint of
Pen & Sword Books Limited
Yorkshire - Philadelphia

ISBN 978 1 47387 5 876

A CIP catalogue record for this book is available from the British Library

Printed and bound in the UK by TJ International, Padstow, Cornwall

Pen & Sword Books Limited incorporates the imprints of Atlas, Archaeology, Aviation, Discovery, Family History, Fiction, History, Maritime, Military, Military Classics, Politics, Select, Transport, True Crime, Air World, Frontline Publishing, Leo Cooper, Remember When, Seaforth Publishing, The Praetorian Press, Wharncliffe Local History, Wharncliffe Transport, Wharncliffe True Crime and White Owl.

For a complete list of Pen & Sword titles please contact
PEN & SWORD BOOKS LIMITED
47 Church Street, Barnsley, South Yorkshire S70 2AS, United Kingdom
E-mail: enquiries@pen-and-sword.co.uk
Website: www.pen-and-sword.co.uk

Or
PEN AND SWORD BOOKS
1950 Lawrence Rd, Havertown, PA 19083, USA
E-mail: Uspen-and-sword@casematepublishers.com
Website: www.penandswordbooks.com

Contents

Acknowledgements

Grateful thanks are due to staff at Glossop Library, Buxton Library, Derby Libraries and Derby County Record Office for their assistance and information; to the editorial and proof reading staff at Pen & Sword for taking the time and trouble to read and evaluate my work, and for their always helpful suggestions; to my two daughters who take a great interest in Derbyshire as their 'home county'; and, last but not least, to my husband, Mike Greenman, for driving me around the county during my research (mostly without complaint) plus finding decent lunchtime stops, cooking meals when I am busy writing, proof reading the finished copy and offering his general support.

Introduction

Derbyshire is a long sprawling county of very different topographical nature from north to south. High Peak in the north comprises the Dark (gritstone) Peak and the White (limestone) Peak. The Dark Peak, as its name suggests, can be forbidding and is mainly high, barren, windswept moorlands, which includes the highest point of the Peak District National Park, Kinder Scout, one of the very few mountains in England and known locally as the 'killer peak.' Chapel-en-le-Frith proclaims itself the 'capital' of the Dark Peak but, in fact, that title really belongs to Glossop in the far north-west of the county. Edale is the starting point of the Pennine Way and the best access point for Kinder Scout. Gritstone changes abruptly to limestone just before the village of Dove Holes, about 5 miles north of Buxton. Buxton, renowned for its spa waters, is the capital of the White Peak, a gentler, greener, more hospitable countryside than that of the Dark Peak, and there are several notable caves and caverns in the area. Castleton has the famous Blue John Cavern, the only known source of Blue John stone in the world. Chesterfield, notable for its crooked church-spire, and once the centre of the Derbyshire coal mining industry, lies to the north east of the county, while Derby itself lies in the flatter southern parts and is a two-hour drive from Glossop. Due to the size of the county there are eight district councils plus the City of Derby, which is a unitary authority, and all of them come under the umbrella of Derbyshire County Council. The largest of the district councils is the Derbyshire Dales, adjoining High Peak, and includes, among others, Matlock/Matlock Bath, Ashbourne, Chatsworth, the 'plague village' of Eyam, Bakewell (famous for its tarts of the same name), Hathersage (where Little John of Robin Hood legend is said to be buried), and Hartington, well-known for Stilton and Buxton Blue cheeses. Although Derby is the county town of Derbyshire, Matlock is now the county administrative centre.

Derbyshire has been home to a wealth of different industries and occupations that have included lead mining and sheep farming (especially in the north-west of the county), underground and opencast coal mining, Sir Richard Arkwright's Industrial Revolution factory complex at Cromford, silk, Royal Derby pottery, Rolls Royce in Derby, limestone quarrying, and the spa waters of Buxton and Matlock Bath for medicinal purposes. The geographical

Dovedale, illustrating the type of countryside in the more rural parts of northern Derbyshire.

location and insular nature of many places within Derbyshire have ensured the survival of old customs such as well dressings, mummers' plays, 'garland days', tup (uncastrated ram) ceremonies, and oak apple celebrations. Derbyshire played its part in the Great War with great effort and enthusiasm, raising war funds, and sending its fair share of young men to the Fronts. The county's Home Front in the Great War had concentrated on back-up support for the troops, manufacturing munitions, ensuring essential industries and services were kept working, and 'keeping the home fires burning'. Derbyshire women did whatever jobs were necessary to ensure that the country kept running and, in addition, grew vegetables, cooked food and made preserves, pickles, jellies and cakes, sewing or knitting clothes and comforts for soldiers (for which they set a record) as well as their own families, cared for children and nursed wounded men. When the Second World War broke out just twenty years later, Derbyshire rallied, confident that it could make the same necessary contributions again. However, this was a very different war. There was the added need to host, educate and care for thousands of children evacuated from industrialised areas, cities and abroad, and, like everywhere else in England, Derbyshire was subject to threats of aerial invasion, aerial bombardment, fatalities, injuries, damage and destruction, as well as the use of chemical warfare, on a hitherto unknown scale. The fanatical determination of the German leader was that England was to be crushed and conquered and it was warfare in unchartered territory which, for the first time, would reach out and touch every single person in the land.

CHAPTER ONE

1939

The Second World War was not entirely unexpected. There had been growing friction in Europe and Hitler played off one power against another as he annexed territories he believed belonged to Germany or should come under German rule. Neville Chamberlain was prime minister and, although he had recognised the danger signs of Hitler's forcing a union with the Austrian government ('Anschluss' as it was known) and his obvious intention to annexe the Sudeten lands (which were then part of Czechoslovakia), he was essentially a man of appeasement and sought talks with Benito Mussolini based on the idea that lessening the tension between Italy and Britain would help to pacify the European situation (Italy had recently invaded and conquered Ethiopia for which the country had been roundly condemned by its European neighbours). The foreign secretary, Anthony Eden, resigned over Chamberlain's move, and was applauded by Winston Churchill for 'standing up against long, dismal, drawling tides of drift and surrender'. The celebratory years in England during the immediate aftermath of the Great War had given way to economic hardship, strikes, hunger marches, and the effects of the Wall Street crash in 1929 which led to the Great Depression of the 1930s. The growth and comparative prosperity of the German nation, the Nuremburg rallies, the gradual stealth by which Germany was helping herself to surrounding territories, made eventual war appear inevitable, despite Chamberlain's policies of appeasement and his government passing a number of Acts in 1937 and 1938 designed to induce a 'feel good factor'. These had included: the Factories Act improving working conditions in factories and cutting working hours for women and children; the Coal Act for nationalising coal deposits; the Holidays with Pay Act which gave workers the right to one week's paid leave per year; and the Housing Act encouraging slum clearances and maintaining rent control. However, it was not a question for most people of 'if', but 'when', war would be declared. In late September 1938 it had briefly seemed as if war would be avoided. Chamberlain had gone to Munich to negotiate with Hitler, believing him when he expressed a desire for eternal peace with Britain and he promised not to invade or annex the whole of

Czechoslovakia. By the end of September Chamberlain had returned with an Anglo-Munich agreement of which he famously declared 'a British Prime Minister has returned from Germany bringing peace with honour. I believe it is peace for our time.'

The annexation of the Sudetenland took place in October 1938, which was followed by the Kristallnacht attacks on German Jews in November 1938 and the invasion of Czech provinces in March 1939. Warning bells were by now ringing in Britain and on 3 June the Military Training Act came into force requiring all men aged 20–21 to be liable for call-up to serve as 'militia men' for a minimum period of four years. It was the first peacetime draft for the country. In the Great War hostilities had commenced after the Germans had invaded Belgium. This time the touch-paper was the German invasion of Poland on 1 September 1939. Two days later, when Britain and France finally declared war on Germany, the overall mood of the British people was of resignation rather than surprise. Neville Chamberlain spoke to the nation in a radio broadcast from the Cabinet Room at 10 Downing Street. He explained that the British ambassador in Berlin had handed the German government a note stating that, unless the Germans gave notice by 11 am on 3 September that they were prepared to withdraw their troops from Poland, Britain and Germany would be at war. Then came the news that everyone had dreaded. 'I have to tell you now,' said Chamberlain in low sombre tones, 'that no such undertaking has been received, and that consequently this country is at war with Germany.' It was certainly not the outcome that the government had wanted but it was the one they had feared and expected. That same day the National Service (Armed Forces) Act was passed meaning that all men aged between 18 and 41 were liable for conscription; followed by the passing of the National Registration act on 7 September which introduced compulsory identity cards.

Oswald Mosley, who had founded the British Union of Fascists during the 1930s, was interned and his infamous Blackshirts (security men as he euphemistically termed them) were disbanded. However, one member of the group, William Joyce, had quietly slipped away to work in Germany. Before leaving England, he had lived unobtrusively in the small north east Derbyshire mining village of Renishaw which lies very close to the Chesterfield Canal, not far from Sheffield. It was this that gave Derbyshire an unwelcome link with one of the stranger episodes of the war when fascism stretched its ugly fingers right into the heart of Britain. Renishaw initially seemed an odd choice by William Joyce for his home, but perhaps not so strange given that Renishaw Hall lay close by. The Hall, the setting for *Lady Chatterley's Lover* (D.H. Lawrence, 1928), was the home of the rather eccentric Sitwell family. Sir George Sitwell, and his children, Dame Edith, Sir Osbert and Sir Sacheverell Sitwell were friends of Mosley and sympathetic to the fascist cause.

William Joyce was a gifted orator 'thin, pale, intense, he had not been speaking many minutes before we were electrified by this man…so terrifying

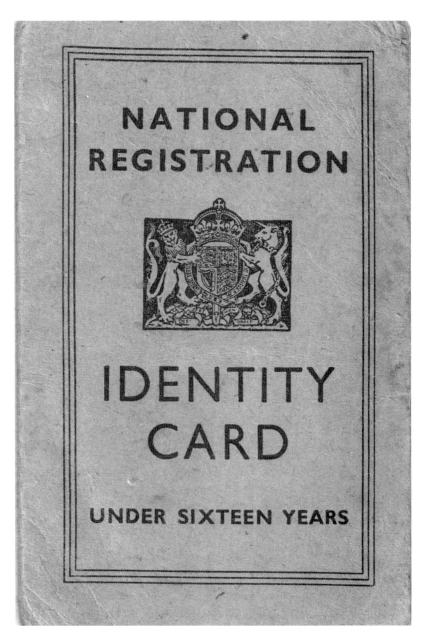

Second World War identity card.

in its dynamic force... so vituperative... so vitriolic' (Cecil Robert, 1932).
Although born in America, Joyce was brought up in Ireland. His father was
an Irish Catholic who had become a United States citizen; his mother was

from Lancashire. Joyce gained a first-class degree from Birkbeck College in London, and he felt his intelligence and his rather unusual persona singled him out for a career in the Foreign Office. When this didn't happen, Joyce became increasingly alienated. During his early twenties, perhaps while still at Birkbeck, he had become interested in fascism and he joined Oswald Mosley's British Union of Fascists (BUF) in 1932. He became the BUF Director of Propaganda but lost his job when Mosley downsized staff after the 1937 election. Joyce had had a dream of Mosley becoming prime minister and of himself becoming Viceroy of India, working under Mosley. Consequently, when the Government of India Bill, designed to allow India more freedom and limited self-government, was passed in 1935, Joyce lost it. He bitterly denounced those who supported the Bill as 'feeble…one loathsome fetid purulent tumid mass of hypocrisy hiding behind Jewish dictators….' Mosley began distancing himself from Joyce as Joyce's hatred of the Jews became more and more paranoid, and, when he wrote his autobiography after the war, William Joyce scarcely merited a mention. Joyce became more and more outspoken, his views more extreme, denouncing the Jews for everything from his failing to complete his MA to all that was wrong in the world. 'I don't regard Jews as a class,' he thundered, 'I regard them as a privileged misfortune.' Blaming Jewish finance for the Second World War he refused to 'fight for Jewry against the Fuhrer….' and fled to Germany with his wife, Margaret, in August 1939, where, in 1940, he officially became a German citizen. He worked for German radio, where his power of oratory and dislike of Britain stood him in good stead. Joyce would later become known as Lord Haw Haw who broadcast regularly against the Allies in general and Britain in particular, applauding their losses, denigrating their achievements, and sneering at their misery, using the call sign 'Germany calling! Germany calling!' Despite his intelligence and education, Joyce still appeared to make the common mistake of confusing socialism with National Socialism. He wanted 'to build something new, something really national, something truly socialist,' but he failed to note the differentiation. Socialism, 'the individual is everything', is centred round the individual and the need for a caring sharing society with equal opportunities for everyone. National Socialism, 'the State is everything,' is centred round the State with benefits only for an autocratic leader or a small oligarchy.

Derbyshire had two regiments fighting in the war: the Sherwood Foresters and the Derbyshire Yeomanry. Both were mobilised from the beginning of the Second World War. The name of the Sherwood Foresters came from the amalgamation in 1881 of the 95th Derbyshire Regiment with the 45th Nottinghamshire Regiment. The Derbyshire Regiment had acquitted themselves well in the Crimean War (1854–1856) and a memorial was built at Crich in Derbyshire to honour the fallen from that war. Although this monument was destroyed by a landslide in 1882, it was rebuilt forty years

Sherwood Foresters Memorial.

later as a memorial to those of the regiment who had fought bravely but were killed in the Great War, to which were added the names of the regimental members who died in the service of their country throughout the Second World War. During the war the regiment fought valiantly in the Norwegian Campaign, at Dunkirk, and in the North African, Middle Eastern and Italian campaigns. There were seventeen battalions in which nearly 27,000 men served, and over 400 battle decorations were won; although 1,500 men from the regiment lost their lives. The 1st Derbyshire Yeomanry was based in Derby. Ironically, the regiment had begun life in 1794 as a home defence regiment, although later metamorphosing into a cavalry regiment, and subsequently undergoing various transformations until it became a part of the Territorial Army. In August 1939 a duplicate 2nd Derbyshire Yeomanry Regiment was formed according to wartime government policy. Members of both regiments fought with great gallantry during the war: the 1st Derbyshire Yeomanry fighting in North Africa (Tunisia); the 2nd Derbyshire Yeomanry fighting at El Alamein during the early part of the war and in Western Europe towards the end; losing just under 100 men, but winning battle honours in the Rhineland and the Reichswald.

On 24 August, the Emergency Powers (Defence) Act had been passed. It was effectively the Second World War version of D.O.R.A. (Defence of the Realm Act) issued for the Great War, and basically allowed the government carte blanche to take whatever action was necessary for the defence of the country, to requisition all necessary supplies and services, to search any premises, and to detain any persons regarded as a threat. This Act was not actually repealed until March 1959, almost fourteen years after the end of the Second World War. Army reservists had been called up and all civil defence workers mobilised. The following day the 'national defence companies' (a voluntary reserve force of former members of the armed services) were ordered to protect 'vulnerable points', especially along the east coast. On 30 August the navy was ordered to battle stations. Children from the cities were evacuated to the country where it was believed they would be in less danger from bombing raids. As early as 1937 the government had been preparing for possible future air raids and the RAF had flown reconnaissance flights to ascertain just how much light was visible from the air and quickly discovered that even small lights, like car sidelights, could be seen quite plainly. Throughout 1938 'black-out rehearsals' had been held, although black-out regulations were not actually imposed until 1 September 1939, two days before the official declaration of war. Derbyshire folk, along with the rest of the country, resigned themselves yet again to the fact that windows and doors had to be covered with dark materials and any light which might help enemy aircraft had to be extinguished or at least darkened. Street lamps were switched off and the use of torches forbidden. Accidents and crime rates rose sharply. In order to reduce accidents folk were told to wear or carry something white and to look out for red lights before stepping off a pavement. The edges of pavements were painted white and people were told to walk slowly on the left-hand side in the dark. White bars were painted on street lampposts, gates, vehicles, and other obstacles. Crimes of burglary, looting and assault were less easy to tackle as the darkness was on the side of the criminal which made chasing or catching them very difficult. It is hard to imagine complete night darkness today but on the remoter British islands, where there is scant population and no street lighting, moonless or cloudy nights can be dark to the extent that, without a torch, the only method is to feel your way by shuffling of feet and/or touch. For most it is a scary and sobering experience.

There was also a sad and rather tragic side effect for animals after the declaration of war. Food rationing had re-awakened a panic about not having enough to eat and being unable to feed cats and dogs as had happened in the Great War. This resulted in a 'pet cull' during the late summer of 1939. In one week 750,000 British pets were killed. Some pet owners, especially those who were compulsorily conscripted into the Armed Forces and had no one to look after their pets, were forced to take this action. One heartbroken owner tearfully apologised to their two-year-old dog who was put to sleep by saying that at least its short life had been happy and that it had given its people a lot of joy. The RSPCA and the Royal Veterinary Corps tried to stop this slaughter, especially as dogs were needed for the war effort; but it was in vain. Widespread panic had prevailed and the wholesale destruction of pets was advised. As one historian, Hilda Kean, put it, 'one of the things people had to do – evacuate the children, put up the black-out curtains, and kill the cat....'

Derbyshire County Council had been issuing air raid and 'black-out' information since the summer of 1938 when Long Eaton (near Derby) was informed it would be taking part in the first 'black-out' exercise organised by the Home Office. Long Eaton Urban District Council and Shardlow Rural District Council were to work together as one district to organise dealing with casualties, first-aid posts, clearance stations and ambulance stations. The two councils would also work in conjunction to 'clear debris from roads and public places, deal with damaged buildings and the rescue of anyone trapped, and decontaminate public places or buildings affected by poison gas....' Information was also issued on how electricity supplies, the LMS railway and local RAF stations would be affected. Plans were also being made for evacuees to be sent to nearby Sawley in the borough of Erewash, although this did not happen until 1944 when twenty-two children from Dagenham and two children from Tottenham were admitted to Sawley National School.

However, for the first eight months of the war there were no major military operations or any aerial attacks on the Western Front until the Germans attacked France and the Low Countries on 10 May 1940. This period was dubbed 'the phoney war' and it lulled everyone into a sense of false security. Many evacuated children returned to their homes and few people bothered with the gas masks they had been warned to always carry with them. There were no exceptions to this rule, even for brides at their wedding. One Derbyshire bride in the autumn of 1939 insisted that the gas masks belonging to her and her bridesmaids should be draped in an attractive material matching their dresses and have horseshoes hung from their respirators in an attempt to make them less threatening and more festive in keeping with her big day. The development of the gas mask was in response to the appalling deaths and injuries from the chlorine gas which had first been introduced by the Germans during the Great War. The masks were made of black leather and had a sinister appearance like that of a science fiction monster with bug eyes, a large flat nose/mouth piece containing a filter, and a tube leading from the side. The supreme irony was that some of the filters used contained blue asbestos which was not realised to be deadly poisonous at that time. Masks for babies encompassed most of the child and must have been quite hot and claustrophobic for the unfortunate infant. Gas masks were enclosed in a small box with straps and strict instructions as to how they should be packed. People were expected to carry their gas masks with them at all times, and they could be punished for not doing so. If they lost their gas mask folk were forced to replace them at their own not inconsiderable expense. By the end of September 1939 some 38 million gas masks had been distributed around the country, but, in the event, they were never needed.

Other lessons learned from the Great War had also been well remembered; although not the foresight for much advance military preparation. Britain's resources were depleted, despite the obvious signs of growing hostility from Germany, and German intelligence was well aware of this fact. The man of the moment in this war was Winston Churchill, but he had also served in the Great War, both in the army and in the government. He had admired much of David Lloyd George's handling of the situation both at home and abroad, and the methods he had used to guide the country through the Great War. Food rationing had been a major issue in the Great War, although it did not start until 1917, but Churchill recognised that it needed to start at the beginning of this war, not towards the end, if stocks and supplies were to be efficiently and effectively conserved and utilised. Derbyshire, being a very rural county in great parts, took this as seriously as they had during the Great War. Anyone who had access to a garden, an allotment, even a public park or other space, began the 'Dig for Victory' process all over again. Initially, at the outbreak of war, the minister of food, Lord Woolton, had ordered that strict minimal daily rations were to be issued to each adult which consisted of:

1lb (0.5kg) potatoes
1oz (0.375g) bread
6oz (0.198g) vegetables

2oz (0.036g) oatmeal
1oz (0.018g) fat
½pt (0.25ltr) milk
No meat

Churchill was horrified by the basic spartan approach of such a diet and ordered Lord Woolton to adopt more generous rations immediately. While Churchill was all in favour of food rationing he recognised that people needed a basic daily minimum intake of nutrition if they were to work efficiently and make a proper contribution to the war effort. Nevertheless, a meal designed for Derbyshire school children in 1934, and known as the 'Glossop Health Sandwich', was re-introduced. This consisted of 3oz (0.054g) of wholemeal bread spread with ¾oz (0.0135g) margarine and a filling containing ¾oz (0.0135g) of salad, 1.5oz (0.027g) of cheese, ¾oz (0.0135g) brewer's yeast (a rich source of vitamin B12), and a little fresh fruit or chopped parsley. Lord Woolton relented a little. He admitted that there were plenty of supplies of bread, potatoes and vegetables, but he warned that meat, cheese, bacon and eggs were in short supply and that they would remain so. The British have always been keen meat eaters, but meat was rationed from the end of September, and Lord Woolton was keen to promote a more vegetarian approach. He therefore encouraged the use of vegetarian cookery and developed his own 'Woolton pie' recipe which consisted of carrots, parsnips, potatoes, and turnips in oatmeal, with a potato or pastry crust and served with brown gravy. It was decidedly unpopular, probably due to the fact that it contained only root vegetables and was rather dry. The addition of a few herbs (which were not rationed), fried onions, and the brown gravy, perhaps thickened by the oatmeal, within the pie might have made it more palatable.

In the Derbyshire winters, which could be bitterly cold, with often heavy snowfall on the hills, warming food was essential. Hotpots, pan haggerty, Irish colcannon, thick warming soups and dumplings, were popular, as well as a lot of bread. The midday meal for those working in the Derbyshire mills, mines and manufactories, was usually sandwiches, since they could be eaten 'in situ'. During the Great War, Glossop, for one, had requested extra rations of butter/margarine for this reason, but it quickly became obvious that this would not happen in the present war. Meat and potato pie, served with red cabbage, has also long been a Derbyshire favourite, although during the Second World War this became just potato pie. Its popularity, however, continued long after the war was over, and even today (2018) potato pie suppers are still popular in Derbyshire pubs on quiz nights. Bread, although not actually rationed until after the war was over, became one of the most contentious wartime foods. Lord Woolton had also insisted that white bread must be replaced with a 'national loaf', a type of brown wholemeal bread which was dismissed as 'mushy and grey' and was fairly universally disliked. A lad from Crich described the effects of rationing. Fruit and sweets began to disappear from the shops. Ration books for use at the butchers, bakers and grocers came into force and the coupons they contained were date stamped for when they could be used. Young children had green ration books for extra milk, orange juice, and cod liver oil, the latter being almost universally disliked. The lad's father had two pigs and when one was killed, the Ministry of Food took half and the family had ham, bacon and pork from the other half; but they had to give up their bacon, meat and fat rations until all their own meat was eaten. This particular lad didn't eat meat so, to his great delight, he was given two slices of fried bread for breakfast each day. As in the Great War, the villages and rural areas of Derbyshire fared a little better during food rationing than the urban areas and the towns. Certain fruit and vegetables were grown and sold around the villages. One man from Melbourne near Derby grew and sold cabbages and cauliflowers; while another just sold cress and watercress. Tomatoes were grown and sold in Whatstandwell. Turnips and potatoes were grown in Crich, and a local house had a large pear tree whose fruit was sold to the children. Natural resources were more readily available and there was a greater potential for growing fruit and vegetables, keeping hens, and obtaining fresh milk literally straight from the local cows. Blackberries, elderberries, wild raspberries and crab apples grew in the hedgerows; while rabbits and birds were often available for the pot. One small boy, evacuated to Hathersage in the Peak District, recalled that, in the family with whom he was billeted, the lady of the house did all her own cooking and preserving, and she also kept hens, so that there never seemed to be any shortage of food. Rabbits and hares were not covered by food rationing regulations and in rural Derbyshire there was no shortage of them.

Petrol rationing was also introduced from 23 September. 'Motor spirit', as petrol was then called, was rationed by coupons allowing so many units per month depending upon the size of the engine. At this time one unit equalled one gallon (just under 4ltrs). Again, this hit Derbyshire hard because of the rural nature of much of the county. A table was published showing petrol rationing limits:

- for cars up to 7 horse power 4 units or gallons per month
- for cars 8-9 horse power 5 units or gallons per month
- for cars up to 10-12 horse power 6 units or gallons per month
- for cars up to 13-15 horse power 7 units or gallons per month
- for cars up to 16-19 horse power 8 units or gallons per month
- for cars 20 horse power and upwards 10 units or gallons per month.

The month didn't end well for many. On 27 September the first war tax was levied as well as an increase in income tax. The prices of food and petrol were also increasing in addition to extra taxes and the 'financial squeeze' was beginning to hit hard.

It had been obvious to most people in the summer of 1939 that war was coming, but hard to believe that it would actually happen, so, as far as possible, it was a case of business as usual. The Labour Movement in Derbyshire was quite active and this year the Transport and General Workers' Union (TGWU) had chosen the Derbyshire Dales village of Youlgreave as the place for their summer quarterly meeting. It was well-dressing week in Youlgreave, an ancient annual custom of thanksgiving for a good supply of clean water, in much the same vein as harvest thanksgiving celebrates a good harvest and sufficient food for the coming year. The wells were dressed with a topical design, etched on soft clay, into which the petals of freshly picked flowers had been pressed. Derby trades unionists had become very apprehensive about the immediate threat of war and the infiltration of fascism into some of the higher echelons of British society. The Derby Joint Engineering Trades were utterly opposed to the conscription they knew would come if war was declared, while the Derby branch of the distributive trades union, NUDAW, feared war would bring lower wages and redundancies. It was barely twenty years since the Armistice which had ended the Great War and many workers, or a member of their families, had served in that war and could well remember the chaos, the problems and the austerity which had resulted.

When war was finally declared many union members actually joined up voluntarily, others were conscripted. However, the trades unions decided that none of their members should be penalised in any way for offering their services to their country and insisted that they be allowed to retain union membership while undertaking national service. Determined to protect their interests, the unions insisted on a raft of actions and initiatives. Most important of these was the provision of air-raid shelters. British Celanese, which manufactured acetate fibres and acetic acid at their plant in Spondon, Derby, had led the way by installing shelters even before war had been declared. Once the war had started and numbers of union members had gone to do their duty for king and country, it left the remaining union members in a very strong bargaining position since there were less members to do more work, most of which was essential for the war effort or keeping the home fires burning. At Derby Paintworks NUDAW members obtained a 10 per cent cost of living increase in their wages, and the Co-op Laundry workers also obtained a good settlement for lost earnings due to air raids. The TGWU, the largest union, won decent wage settlements for its members working at Cox's Leadworks, DP Batteries, Celanese Weavers, and a half dozen other firms in and around Derby. The arguments were the same as in the Great War: rising cost of living and keeping a roof over one's head; increased food and fuel prices; austerity and inflation. Those serving in Armed Forces had no bargaining power and their wages remained low. Going on strike for them was regarded as an act of treason for which the penalty could be death. There was resentment. Some said going on strike in wartime was simply greedy and unpatriotic. Others said that they were simply trying to provide for their families and protect their absent colleagues' interests. It was an insoluble situation.

An evacuation programme of children and adults had begun on 1 September before war was even officially declared. Operation Pied Piper (named, so it was said, after the Pied Piper of Hamelin) was responsible for the evacuation of 1½ million people. Manchester evacuated 20,000 of its own children (followed by a further 6,000 from the Channel Islands in 1940) to places in Derbyshire like Buxton, Hathersage, Chinley, Chapel-en-le-Frith, Matlock and Great Hucklow. St James' School in Derby were evacuated to nearby Chellaston while St Joseph's School in Normanton were sent out to Ripley. The children arrived, often tired, hungry and frightened, each clutching a small suitcase, their gas-mask boxes and a favourite doll or teddy bear. Every child had a label tied on around their neck stating their name, age, and home town. The culture shock of moving from city to country could be quite severe and, in some cases, inner-city children found it very hard to adapt to rural life. However, others blossomed and did not want to return to their city homes at all, complaining of overcrowding within their own family plus a lack of privacy and freedom. There was also the question of education. Evacuees would join the village schools in their evacuation area, but a number of parents expressed great concern that education in rural areas was not as good as in the cities and some parents took their children home again so that they could benefit from what was seen as superior education. It worked the other way as well with some parents dismissive of 'book learning'. A lot of the evacuees from urban areas found life out in the Derbyshire countryside quite a fascinating experience. Many had never seen farm animals in the flesh and had no idea where the foods they ate came from or how they were prepared for the table. Although a number of children returned to their homes as a result of the 'phoney war', there were numerous concerns for their safety and many returned to their 'foster' homes.

Shortly before the war, the armed forces had begun looking for suitable sites to store weapons, ammunition, and bombs. The main requirements were that such locations should be remote; difficult to pinpoint from the air; and close to a railway line where there was room for sidings and a marshalling yard. Disused mines in remote locations, because of their nature, were often favoured to reduce accessibility by the flying capacity of German planes. The problem was that there was a general lack of availability of such sites. There had been an artillery range during the Great War on Harpur Hill, just outside Buxton, and, shortly before the outbreak of the Second World War, the RAF were viewing the site with considerable interest for various reasons.

Sorrow Quarry on Harpur Hill was a quarry worked out by the time of the Second World War. Prior to that it had been worked by the Buxton Limestone Firm and then by ICI Ltd. It was also well camouflaged and often shrouded in mists. The geology had been proved to be suitable for building underground

IUXTON GENERAL VIEW FROM THE SLOPES   28871

Buxton around the time of the Second World War.

storage resources for ammunition of many types and existing quarrying activities would disguise building activity from aerial reconnaissance. The quarry waste could then be used to give additional surface cover to the underground features. Furthermore, there were good railway connections to the area. Objections were raised by a number of people, including the Duke of Devonshire, because of the site's proximity to Buxton which, at that time, was still a spa town. However, the Air Ministry was determined and the site was approved in 1938, although the RAF did not take it over until December 1939. Its official name was RAF Maintenance Unit 28 and it remained in constant use until 1960 when the RAF abandoned the site.

The construction of the tunnels was always going to be difficult given the nature of the site, because the quarry varied in depth from 60ft (18.3m) to 80ft (24.4m) and the shape was irregular. It would prove to be very costly and totally impractical to create a uniform shape for a neat block of tunnels, so they had to be built within the quarry's natural distorted 'S' shaped confines. This created immense engineering difficulties and an impossible geometrical complexity for supporting roof arches at the two points where the quarry curved. Part of the specification included two entrances and a standard-gauge railway line running right through the complex; but the quarry's natural 'S' shape made the idea of a through railway line virtually impossible. Finally, it was decided upon a single-storey structure 16ft (5m) high with an arched stone roof and an overhead backfill of lime waste 42ft (12.8m) deep to align with the natural ground level. A central tunnel would house the railways with three storage tunnels running off each side accessed through archways at 90ft (27.4m) intervals. The slope of the quarry floor would also enable a basement under the two easternmost tunnels with two electric lifts and a ramp for ease of access. Careful consideration was also given to air conditioning and ventilation for the whole complex, but this idea was virtually abandoned because the ammunition did not really require these measures for stability.

Alfred McAlpine Ltd took responsibility for the construction, but suffered numerous setbacks. The weather in the winter of 1939–1940 was atrocious. Rain fell almost continually and heavy snowfall blocked road and railway for nearly a fortnight in late January and early February. The first train carrying supplies to get through after the snow was then derailed when the rails sank into the mud. The complex opened in March 1940, before completion; but the rail tunnel was only 12ft (3.7m) high instead of the standard 13ft 6ins (4.1m) which meant lowering the track floor by cutting through solid concrete. Further problems followed. The overhead backfill was only 20ft (6m) deep at this point and RAF reconnaissance flights revealed the complex was visible from the air. Orders were given immediately to increase the overhead backfill at once to a depth of 42ft (12.8m). However, it was discovered that the weight of overfill, as at Llanberis, a similarly large subterranean ammunition stores in Wales, could cause cracks and threaten collapse of the roof. While it was being decided how to tackle this problem there was a roof collapse at Llanberis which buried an ammunitions supply train. Fortunately, no one was killed or seriously hurt, but it took some time to clear up the resulting mess. Checks were now carried out as a matter of urgency at Harpur Hill and some similar cracks were discovered which resulted in the need to rebuild and strengthen the roof arches. The same aerial reconnaissance had shown that supply and ammunition trains were also highly visible, so it was then immediately ordered that deliveries of supplies and ammunitions should only take place after dark, and this usually took longer than in daylight.

As if these weren't problems enough they were followed by allegations of possible subversion and sabotage by Irish workers on the site. This was based on unsubstantiated allegations made about Irish labour at the underground defence site in Corsham which was also being constructed by Alfred McAlpine Ltd. McAlpines were using Irish labour because most eligible English labour had been conscripted into the armed forces. As a result, MI5 undertook a discreet investigation into the Irish staff at Harpur Hill but their covert activities failed to turn up any real evidence. The security forces were edgy, however, because it had been decided to store chemical weapons and mustard gas in the basement area of Harpur Hill, with bombs and other ammunition in the tunnels above and, of course, most on-site workers would have known this.

Conventional, biological and chemical weapons were all stored in the series of tunnels or galleries built beneath Harpur Hill; it was the largest ammunition store in England. Llanberis in Wales was the only other wartime

Entrance to one of the underground tunnels in Harpur Hill, Buxton.

ammunitions store equal in size. There may eventually have been up to eleven tunnels within Harpur Hill, each said to be approximately 25ft (7.6m) high by 17ft (5.1m) wide by half a mile (804m) long. Bombs, incendiaries, explosives and chlorine or mustard gas were stored here. The gas was both unstable and corrosive and eventually the decision was taken to remove it from underground storage. The village of Harpur Hill is situated close by, at the foot of Harpur Hill. It is quite a large village with a church, school, shops, a pub, and several rows of streets. It is probably unlikely the inhabitants were told what lay beneath their feet in the Second World War; mainly for reasons of national security, but also to avoid widespread panic. It was absolutely imperative that the Germans should never discover what Harpur Hill really contained; and they obviously never learned the truth for they made no deliberate attempt to attack the place and the town of Buxton was largely ignored by German bombers. There were a couple of lucky escapes. In 1941 a German Luftmine or parachute mine, which had probably been jettisoned after attacks on Manchester, landed on Upper Midhope Moors. The second rather more serious incident occurred on Christmas Eve in 1944 when a stray and deadly V-1 cruise missile fell close to Black Edge near Buxton. No real damage was caused in either case but if the V-1 (V for vengeance according to the Germans) had landed on Harpur Hill the outcome could have been quite catastrophic.

All cinemas were closed in September but soon reopened as the government realised the need for some sort of entertainment and escape from everyday problems. They also realised that cinemas could be used to promote their own propaganda and a number of short films and documentaries were made for this purpose. Football was badly affected as well, and initially

Quarry 'hummocks' on Harpur Hill, Buxton, disguising the underground tunnels built beneath to store ammunition in the Second World War.

professional football was suspended. Although football grounds reopened in September, those watching games were usually limited to 8,000 spectators. Radio, cinema and dances were the main forms of entertainment, but in many parts of rural Derbyshire this narrowed down to just radio, and those who had time read a great deal as well. Margaret Mitchell's classic story of the American civil war, *Gone with the Wind*, was made into a film in 1939 starring Clark Gable and Vivien Leigh. It was the most popular film of the Second World War. Radio though was generally the chief form of entertainment and news. The BBC had just two programmes, the Home Service (today's equivalent is Radio 4) and the Forces Programme. Singer Vera Lynn, known as the Forces' Sweetheart, was one of the most popular entertainers, with songs like the 'The White Cliffs of Dover' and 'We'll Meet Again'. The BBC news was the main means of communication of events for many people. Much of it was war news of air raids, land and sea battles, plus the general progress of the war, although there was some home front news as well. By 1945 there were 10 million radio licences held in Britain. Wartime radios were quite cumbersome in comparison to modern sets. The sets were worked by valves and enclosed in polished wooden cases with the speaker covered in a kind of hessian. There were usually just two knobs on the front, one for volume and on/off facilities, with the other used to search for radio stations.

The cancellation of Guy Fawkes celebrations in November disappointed Derbyshire children who had looked forward to building up a bonfire, making the guy, and watching him burn; then having a few fireworks, while potatoes were baked in the embers of the fire. Now Christmas was to be a muted affair for the whole country during this first year of the war. The authorities were keen to prevent what they termed frivolous spending when Britain needed every penny for the war effort. There was a campaign to encourage folk to put into war savings whatever they would have spent on Christmas presents. This was never going to achieve a 100 per cent success rate, but people did reduce their spending on gifts and Christmas decorations. Before the war many of the toys on sale in Britain had been imported from Germany. This had ceased abruptly, and although the Primrose League made efforts to establish a British toy industry to benefit from what had been a lucrative market for the Germans, most toys during the war were either homemade or made from recycled materials. Even in peacetime there was not the expectation, as there is in the twenty-first century, of multiple and very expensive gifts to order. Many children were content with two or three small gifts, an orange and a few sweets. External Christmas lights were banned due to the black-out and internal ones were discouraged because of the need to conserve energy materials. There was a paper shortage and consequently there were very few Christmas decorations on sale. Children made their own paper chains by collecting scraps of paper, cutting them into strips and gluing them together in interlocking circles. Christmas cards were not large or flamboyant, or even made of card. They were small, often home decorated, and on flimsy poor-quality paper. However, it was very much the thought that counted, and those serving in the armed forces treasured their Christmas messages from loved ones without caring too much about the materials on which they were written. There were few luxury foodstuffs due to rationing and turkeys were out of the question. Coupons were saved, and the main festive dishes were either chicken or ham. In rural Derbyshire these might have been supplemented by rabbits or a brace of birds. However, not even Hitler could stop the carol concerts or the pantomimes which were celebrated in churches and schools in every town and village in the land. The BBC initiated a special Christmas Day programme on the radio in 1939 and, for the first time, this included a special Christmas broadcast by King George VI. The Christmas broadcasts by the sovereign to his subjects proved so popular that they were continued after the war was over and when the king died in 1952 his daughter, now Queen Elizabeth II, continued the tradition and has done so right up to the present day (2018).

CHAPTER TWO

1940

Early in 1940 the Norway Campaign, a naval-based campaign by the Allies to seize Norway which was a neutral country, took place. The 8th Battalion of the Sherwood Foresters were involved in this campaign. It was foiled by the Germans in early April when they unexpectedly occupied Denmark and invaded Norway, forcing Allied troops to withdraw. The 8th Battalion then faced a difficult and dangerous retreat through deep snow in mountainous terrain, with crack ski troops chasing them and, inevitably, there were a number of casualties. Neville Chamberlain did not head a unified coalition government because neither Clement Attlee and the Labour Party nor David Lloyd George and the Liberals would support him. Attlee did not agree with him and Lloyd George was quite hostile, especially over the matter of his appeasement policies. The post-mortem debate on Norway began on 7 May, and on 9 May Hitler invaded the Low Countries. The 'phoney war' was over and Chamberlain finally realised that it was time for him to go. On 10 May he resigned as prime minister and advised the king to send for Winston Churchill who, as First Lord of the Admiralty, had been involved with naval battles during the period of the phoney war. By this time Chamberlain was not receiving a good press due to public perception that he was too trusting, perhaps too naïve, and had 'been played' by Hitler to Britain's detriment; in addition to the mishandling of the Norway campaign and other early wartime matters. The whole business of powerful criticism and losing power depressed Chamberlain deeply, and his reputation was tarnished by what was now seen as his over eagerness to appease Germany instead of seeking other alliances and making more preparations for possible war. Neville Chamberlain died on 9 November 1940 almost six months to the day after his resignation from the premiership.

Between 26 May and 4 June the legendary evacuation of Dunkerque (Dunkirk) took place. A British Expeditionary Force (BEF) had been sent to defend France but, after German forces invaded France, Belgium and Holland on 10 May, the BEF found itself trapped on the northern coast of France and withdrew to Dunkerque, the nearest reasonable port. The 2nd, 1/5th, 2/5th and 9th battalions of the Sherwood Foresters were part of the BEF and fought bravely alongside their colleagues. However, the BEF was ultimately defeated, losing 68,000 soldiers to the French campaign along with most of its tanks and armoury; although a kind of victory was snatched from the jaws of defeat by the rescue of 338,226 soldiers from the beaches of Normandy, using a flotilla of 800 boats of all shapes and sizes working alongside military craft. Churchill called their rescue 'a miracle of deliverance' but he warned against regarding Dunkerque as a victory.

On 10 June Italy, under the leadership of Benito Mussolini, joined the war on the side of Germany. There were a number of Italian communities in England. The Italians were sociable people who had integrated well with their English neighbours. Some had married English girls and taken on British citizenship. Numbers of them had served in the Great War with the British forces so it came as a great shock to discover that suddenly they were the enemy. Where before there had been only welcome and friendliness there were now riots against the 'Italian enemies'. Churchill saw them all as a national security threat and ordered internment of every Italian male aged between 17 and 60. The men were arrested and taken away, leaving their wives and children in tears without any form of support. Some of them even had sons serving in the British army. Despite their protestations of loyalty all Italian men were questioned about their loyalties and if they supported the 'Fascisti'. The answers given appear to have been irrelevant because they were all interned.

In some respects, Derbyshire was an ideal county for prisoner of war (PoW) camps in the Second World War. There were many remote locations with scant communications and a lack of transport facilities. It was intended that PoWs should work for the benefit of their captors and there was plenty of

Stoney Middleton, site of a Second World War PoW camp.

quarrying and farming work to be done in Derbyshire. Camps held prisoners of various nationalities, Italians, Germans, Russians, etc., and there were a number of PoW camps in the county.

These included Dove Holes; Stoney Middleton; The Hayes at Swanick; Nether Heage Camp in Belper; New Drill Hall at Clay Cross; Alvaston Park; Allerton; Oaks Green at Sudbury; Weston camp at Weston on Trent and King's Newton. Today there is often little trace left of these camps. Clay Cross New Drill Hall, used by the Sherwood Foresters prior to the First World War, became a PoW camp in the Second World War, but it has long since been demolished. Clay Cross is an industrial and mining area and today the site of the New Drill Hall is occupied by an industrial estate. The Dove Holes camp was small and only housed Italians living in England who were interned on Churchill's orders after Italy had joined the war on the side of the Germans. There are eyewitness accounts of them being allowed to visit nearby Buxton at weekends; distinguishable by their prison camp uniforms of brown battledress with PoW emblazoned on them. Oaks Green in Sudbury was built as a military hospital for the United States Air Force but became a PoW camp in the Second World War. In 1948, some might say appropriately enough, it was adapted for use as a civilian prison. It is now known as HMP Sudbury and is a Category D male prison. Consequently, exploration of the site is not possible.

Stoney Middleton was quite a remote industrial village during the Second World War, whose main occupation was quarrying limestone used for construction, road-building and supplying the tarmac plant in Darlton Quarry. Fluorspar, a mineral produced from limestone, was also essential for steel manufacture. The camp was initially built as a military camp on land between

Site of former PoW camp at Stoney Middleton in the Second World War.

Stoney Middleton and Calver and was manned by the Lancashire Fusiliers. It had searchlights and machine guns for protection of the local quarries. Troop quarters were provided in Nissen huts. The reasons for it becoming a PoW camp are unclear but, as initially it housed mainly Italian PoWs, it may have been in response to Churchill's order for the internment of all Italian males in the summer of 1940. Beds provided in PoW camps were often palliasses (straw mattresses), although in this case there were wooden bunk beds for the use of the prisoners. Cooking and washing facilities were adequate, if a little basic, and the Italian PoWs, like their Manchester counterparts, put on a brave and positive face, determined to remain cheerful and make the best of things. They cooked their own meals, kept themselves and their surroundings reasonably clean, and were allowed to attend Mass on Sundays. They worked in the local quarries, their chief task being to break the limestone into small manageable pieces. Although most interned Italians faced hostility at first for being 'the enemy', most of them had been born and brought up in Britain and their fathers had fought for Britain in the Great War. They felt no alliance with either Germany or the Nazis, and a number of them were secretly relieved that, being interned, they could not be sent to fight in the war. Gradually, with their friendly natures and dark good looks, they came to be accepted by local people, and proved themselves adept at craft work, making jewellery for the women and toys for the children. Later, German and a few Austrian PoWs arrived and they generally worked in the quarries or on the local farms. Most of the German PoWs were just ordinary soldiers, some as frightened of the Nazi High Command as anyone else, and a few of them even made friends with their English captors. Today there is no trace at all left of this camp and a small modern housing estate stands on the site which lies by the side of the busy A623 road.

The Hayes in Swanwick, a country house built in mid-Victorian times, is now a Christian conference centre, but it was a PoW camp during the Second World War. Its main claim to fame is the daring story of a small group of German PoWs, calling themselves Swanwick Excavations Inc., who tunnelled their way out by digging a 30m tunnel beneath the building in 1940. Their leader was Franz von Werra, a Messerschmitt pilot who had been forced to crash-land his plane and was subsequently captured. His story reads like something from a *Boy's Own* annual. After his initial capture he absconded from a PoW camp in the Lake District and roamed the countryside freely for five days before he was recaptured and sent to Swanwick. On arrival he was given a single room in the 'Garden House'. Still determined to escape, he and four others tunnelled from a disused bedroom at the rear of the Garden House under the foundations and the surrounding barbed-wire fence; this work took about four weeks. Five days before Christmas all five crawled through the tunnel to freedom. It was bitterly cold, they were ill prepared, they had no money or documents, and four of the group were quickly recaptured. Von

Werra, however, had already made some sort of a plan and he managed to stay free a little longer before being recaptured. After being punished with a spell in solitary confinement he was sent with other prisoners to Canada. Once there he escaped yet again and fled to the USA which was still neutral. After a great deal of legal wrangling on both sides, he was finally allowed to fly back to Germany via Spain, becoming the only German captured in England who managed to escape and return to Germany; and he took with him important information on British interrogation methods. For his escape and his contribution to German Intelligence he was awarded the honour of the Knight's Cross as a hero of the Third Reich. Subsequently, after a short spell serving on the Eastern Front, Von Werra was eventually killed in October 1941 when his plane crashed during a routine North Sea patrol exercise. His body has never been found. The external part of the tunnel was rediscovered during building alterations at The Hayes long after the war was over. Today it remains sealed off by a door bearing an explanatory plaque; and a film, *The One that Got Away* was made telling the story of Von Werra's incredible adventures.

The trades unions were active in Derby and were very anxious that their members should not be penalised by being called up for conscription and that they should retain full union privileges. This was the case in many other parts of the country, but there seemed to be a rash of strikes (900 minor ones during the first months of the war), despite the fact that Churchill had banned strikes at the beginning of the war under order 1305 which was reinforced in 1941 by the Essential Work Order. Ernest Bevin, leader of the Transport and General Workers Union (TGWU), was the Minister of Labour and National Service.

The Hayes, Swanick, c1940s.

In the spring of 1940 agricultural workers in Derbyshire were awarded a minimum weekly wage of 48*s* (£120 at current values) which, while low by modern standards, was a great improvement. Derby itself had a number of industries besides Rolls Royce, including the railways, mining, engineering, textiles and chemical works. There were a further ten wage settlements at companies in and around Derby including the cleaners at Rolls Royce, DP Battery, the engineering workers and the Railway Workshops. The Railway Workshop employees were now on £2.8..0*d* (£120.00) which brought them into parity with Derbyshire agricultural workers who were some of the best paid in the country. In April 1940 fifty tunnel workers, building a new drainage system for Derby demanded a 12½ per cent pay rise on the threat of going on strike, although they were already earning more than the national average. This caused a great deal of dissent and there were 'disturbances' to which the police were called. The project must have been urgent and badly needed because many municipal works were put on hold until after the war. Agricultural workers in Derbyshire, who had their wage rises around this time, also gained a forty-eight hour week, the shortest working hours they had ever had. It was no wonder that membership of the National Union of Agricultural Workers (NUAW) tripled during the war years. Textiles were beginning to suffer as they had in the Great War. Ilkeston Hosiery Union, concerned about labour restrictions, refused to lift a ban on Saturday afternoon working. There seemed to be a general slump in mid-1940 with British Celanese in Derby on short time and two brickworks temporarily closed down. During the summer of 1940 another six groups gained wage settlements including the chemical and textile workers, but despite this the mining and engineering industries remained vulnerable to strikes. However, due to the essential nature of these industries for the war and the reduction in staff caused by conscription, union members were in a strong bargaining position and won some considerable concessions. To compensate some employers tried to increase working hours only to find themselves head-to-head with the unions and forced to back down. The Derby TGWU had been deeply unhappy that the government had refused to amend the Trade Dispute and Trade Union Act 1927, and a strongly worded resolution had been dispatched in March 1940:

> *...this meeting of delegates, representing over six thousand members, emphatically protest against your decision not to amend the Trades Dispute and Trades Union Act 1927, and further, this decision has caused profound distrust of your sincerity in regards to the hard won rights of the Trade Unionists in this country...*

This was endorsed by the Derby branch of NUDAW adding further condemnation by declaring in a resolution that the government was keen 'in conscripting labour but not wealth' and demanding an end to the means test for unemployment assistance. As in the Great War the whole question of unions, workers' rights and strikes, remained an unanswerable quandary and, also, as in the Great War, this provoked more criticism from those serving in the Armed Forces who couldn't strike for more pay and from those who were already desperately economising to help the war effort. The strikers, condemned as greedy and thoroughly unpatriotic by the *Daily Mail,* argued that they simply needed decent wages in order to survive and that they had a duty to protect remuneration and conditions for those away fighting in the war.

The mining industry, which was prevalent in South Derbyshire, was particularly vulnerable to strikes but, in order to understand the sort of life that the miners faced, the National Coal Mining Museum near Wakefield has preserved a coal mine which the public can visit to experience just how miners lived and worked. It is a terrifying learning curve which renders the word 'respect' quite inadequate. About twenty people are crammed into a wire cage measuring little more than 6ft (180cm) x 4ft (120cm) which descends jerkily 550ft (around 170m) down into the earth. There is no electric light. Each person is given a miner's light which is the only illumination. Cameras, phones and watches have to be left at the surface. It is dark, dirty, dank, damp, and smells incredibly musty; water drips down the walls of the shaft. Once in the mine there are lots of long narrow passages in which it is impossible for people over 5ft (150cm) tall to stand upright. At the coalface miners often had to sit or crouch to work the coal from the rock. Battered wooden doors were kept closed between each section to minimise the spread of fire risk. The rock presses in on all sides and air quality sometimes fluctuates which can leave folk hot and breathless with a pounding heart. Pneumoconiosis (known as 'black lung' by miners), is a dust-based lung disease which was an occupational and fatal hazard for miners. In the Great War, mining versus trench warfare was a choice between the lesser of two evils. The miners had an amazing camaraderie with each other and probably a higher chance of survival than those in the trenches; but there is no freedom underground. In the Second World War mining had largely ceased to be even a choice.

Although women were once again doing many of the men's jobs, they did not get the same pay for the same work and this lack of equality led to further protest. By the end of the following year the minimum wage in the Derby Wages Committee area was £3 (£135) for men, while for women it was only £2 (£90). Three days paid holiday for everyone were also included. The women of Derbyshire were reacting to this new war in pretty much the same way as they had reacted to the Great War. They knew it was their job to keep the home fires burning, as the popular slogan went, to cook good meals from scant ingredients, to work in their gardens or on allotments, 'digging for victory' as Churchill had asked them to do, and growing as much food as they could, caring for their children, and helping in some way with the war effort. From 1941 female conscription meant that women were also conscripted into work in factories. However, large numbers of men were free with their complaints if their wives were out working. Dinner would not be on the table when they returned home. The home was not as they would like it. Their children were being fed from tins and not being looked after or disciplined properly. Even worse, some women might be earning more than their husbands and, in the men's eyes, this was shameful indeed. The resulting exhaustion and stress suffered by many women was hardly noticed.

Churchill was very keen on Lloyd George's idea of national kitchens, which had proved a great success in the First World War, and the idea was revived early in 1940. Initially they were called community kitchens until Churchill renamed them British Kitchens or Restaurants. The concept was the same as in the Great War. The kitchens could bulk buy fresh foods at cost and cook cheap nourishing meals on a small number of industrial cookers. This saved money on individual food purchases and the fuel for running individual cookers. Each kitchen had a restaurant attached which was decently furnished. Customers could buy a meat-and-two-vegetables main course followed by a pudding for the modern equivalent of £1. Meals would be simple but quite palatable. Spam with mashed potato, hotpot, stew, pie and mash, baked potatoes, curry (of anything, curried carrots were a favoured dish) and rice, greens in season, with maybe a rice or suet pudding to follow. This meant that busy working people could afford one good square meal a day and it was also intended to remove some of the burden from the shoulders of working women. Beeston was the first 'communal feeding centre' to open, and Long Eaton quickly followed suit by opening a 'municipal restaurant' on Cross Street. In the city of Derby and larger towns like Chesterfield, Glossop and Buxton. These 'communal kitchens/restaurants' proved to be a good idea, but the principle was rather impractical for the villages, which had limited clientele, and in the more rural areas of Derbyshire. Due to the isolation of many homes, petrol rationing and the lack of public transport, the WVS, together with various local and parochial organisations, encouraged many Derbyshire women to sew and knit 'comforts' for the troops in their own homes. Raw materials were provided and the women gave their time and their skills. 'Comforts' covered a wide range of items including socks, helmets, caps, balaclavas, comforters (a type of long scarf), scarves, gloves, wrist warmers, pullovers, cardigans, 'tank tops', nightwear, underwear, shirts, blankets, etc. There were lots of different styles, sizes and colours but 'Comforts' could be knitted in Forces' colours as well: Army – dark or light brown wool; Royal Navy – navy blue; RAF – blue/grey.

One of the most defining effects of the Second World War in Derbyshire were the sheer number of plane crashes, mostly in the Dark Peak but also in the White Peak and other parts of the Pennines. The majority of them were due to bad weather, inexperienced pilots and the unreliability of altimeters at that time. Many of the aircrew survived although a number were killed.

Those who attempted crash-landings often escaped, albeit some with injuries. In May 1940 a pilot flying from Duxford in Cambridgeshire up to Kirkbride got lost and when his fuel ran low he ditched his plane, a Tudor K3308, at the Edale end of Barber Booth. He was unhurt but the plane was badly damaged. At the end of July another pilot crash-landed his plane in Darley Dale after becoming disorientated in poor weather and walked away unhurt, although his plane, a Magister Mk.I N3811, was a 'write-off'. In early September, another disorientated pilot, low on fuel, crash-landed his Spitfire Mk.I P9563 in a field near the cheese producing village of Hartington and escaped unhurt. So too did a pilot in mid-November who crash-landed his Blenheim Mk.I L6800 in a field close to Monyash after becoming lost in low cloud. In early December the two occupants of a Blenheim Mk.I K7172 crash-landed in bad weather at Woolley Bridge in Glossop and both survived. Not so lucky were the crew of a Hampden Mk.I L4189 plane who also became lost in cloud and flew straight into the ground at Black Edge near Buxton in late September. The pilot, co-pilot and wireless operator were killed and the air gunner was seriously injured. Four days before Christmas a crew of four lost their lives when their Hampden Mk.I X3154 crashed into Rushup Edge near Chapel-en-le-Frith. They were on a cross-country night navigation exercise and it is thought the altimeter may have either malfunctioned or been misread.

COPYRIGHT
TSL. 6

TIDESWELL CHURCH

LILYWHITE LTD.
BRIGHOUSE

Tideswell Church, an important Derbyshire village, just before the Second World War.

In early May 1940 some 6,000 child evacuees from the Channel Islands had arrived in Manchester prior to the German occupation of the Channel Islands. The city had already evacuated its own children to places in Derbyshire like Buxton, Hathersage, Chinley, Chapel-en-le-Frith, Matlock and Great Hucklow, and now added most of those from the Channel Islands, especially in the Whaley Bridge and Buxton areas. Others went to Stockport and Disley in neighbouring Cheshire. Some Southend children went to Crich, while 600 boys from the Westcliff High School in Southend were sent to the Herbert Strutt School in Belper. The head of Elizabeth College in Guernsey wanted to keep all his pupils together for education purposes, but the number of schoolboys to be accommodated presented problems. Eventually, the junior boys were housed in Great Hucklow (near the Peak District villages of Tideswell, Eyam and Foolow) while the senior boys were settled into a large house at Whitehall near Buxton. Throughout the war, both groups remained in these designated accommodations, and received their education there as well. Evacuations did not always go according to plan, however, and initially Hathersage, which had expected a large number of evacuees from Manchester, was a little nonplussed when only one small boy arrived with his mother. On 7 June, just a month after the Channel Islands children had arrived, 600 children from the vulnerable East Coast port of Lowestoft arrived in Glossop on a teatime train, exhausted, bewildered, and apprehensive, each holding a small suitcase and a gas mask in a box, with many of the smaller ones also clutching a much-loved doll or teddy bear. Every child had a label tied around their neck showing their name, date of birth and home town. They were taken to St Andrew's School in Hadfield for tea and cake followed by a medical examination, supper and billet allocation. Their education was to be undertaken by Padfield Council School and Castle School Hadfield as nearby St Andrew's already had twenty-one evacuees from St Clement's School in Openshaw (a suburb of Manchester). A number of the Lowestoft evacuees were sent to stay with Lady Partington at Talbot House in Glossop. She treated them very fairly but she remained rather distant. Two small and motherless Lowestoft girls were taken by a loving couple in Chesterfield. The village of Crich near Derby took far more than its fair share of evacuees. In 1939, due to fears of a German attack on Rolls Royce in Derby, children living in the area of the factory had been evacuated to Ockbrook near Borrowash in the Erewash district; but the Pear Tree School near Rolls Royce was evacuated to Crich, some 15 miles from Derby in the opposite direction. Although Crich is only 15 miles from Derby there was no bus service, and petrol rationing prohibited the use of other vehicles, so the children did not get to see their parents very often. Later in 1939 the Railway Servants Orphanage Boys were evacuated from Ashbourne Road in Derby to a large old house on Bull Bridge Hill in Crich and also attended Crich School. As the threat of a German invasion increased from May 1940, children living on the East Coast were evacuated inland. Early on 2 June children from a Southend school were evacuated with their teachers to Crich. Lists of clothing the children would need, together with lists of illnesses they had suffered and inoculations they had received were considered mandatory. Siblings were mainly kept together. Crich seemed to be a popular destination, and, as it was largely rural, older children could always help out on the farms.

The acceptance of evacuees was mixed. Many families welcomed them warmly, showing sympathy, empathy and affection towards often frightened homesick children. Others simply didn't want them but were given no choice by local billeting officers. Some saw the children as unpaid labour and made them work hard around the place in which they were billeted. A few were downright hostile to their charges, laying down strict rules and regulations for behaviour and not giving them enough to eat. Standards of living were often different from the children's homes. Several city evacuees expressed amazement at outdoor toilets and the tin bath system of their new temporary homes while others marvelled at indoor bathrooms and toilets as well as the grandeur of some of the bigger houses. Manners and expectations of certain behavioural standards varied considerably as well. Some children had problems, like bed-wetting (mainly caused by fear and homesickness) which put a severe strain on the foster families with whom they were billeted. However, one of the hardest facts for evacuees to accept was the fact that a request to the government for reduced postage for letters written home by evacuated children was refused. In some cases this meant that children could not write very often to their parents due to financial hardship. Although many of the evacuees were children, some adults came with them, mostly parents and teachers, especially from the Channel Islands but there were also a number of Jewish refugees from war-torn Europe who had managed to escape the clutches of the Nazis. Jewish refugees were spread over the whole country but many gravitated towards the Manchester area which had a large Jewish community.

British summer time (BST), the daylight hours saving scheme adopted in 1916, had continued but at the end of 1940 the clocks had not been put back an hour to Greenwich Mean Time (GMT), as was the custom, but had remained on BST. In the spring of this year the clocks were put forward by another hour so that the country was now two hours ahead of GMT. This was dubbed British Double Summer Time (BDST) which remained in force until autumn 1945. In the winter clocks were put back an hour to BST but did not return to GMT until after the war.

The stately homes of Derbyshire and their owners were expected to contribute to the war effort. Chatsworth House, still a large working model of the Edwardian country house style, would have been ideal for use as a barracks, but the 10th Duke of Devonshire cannily realised that a school would cause far less damage than a battalion. He therefore arranged for the house to be used by Penrhos College, which was a public school for girls in Colwyn Bay. The staff of around forty managed to pack up all the Duke's possessions and house contents in eleven days, and the school moved in. The state rooms were used as dormitories and the resulting condensation caused fungus to grow behind the pictures left hanging on the walls. Three hundred girls and their teachers moved into the house for the full six years of the war. Conditions were a little cramped and hot water was scarce but the safety and beautiful surroundings were more than adequate compensation and as part of their war effort the girls grew vegetables in the gardens.

Hardwick Hall, the former home of a well-known and determined Tudor lady, Bess of Hardwick, gave much of its Park and lands over to the military. Barracks and a gymnasium were erected in the grounds for soldiers and also for interned Italian prisoners and there was a guard house at the Blingsby Gate to the estate. In the summer of 1941 the First Parachute Brigade was formed under Brigadier Sir Richard Gale and training for parachutists was undertaken at Hardwick. A parachute jump tower was installed within a periphery of 53 acres south-west of the Hall leased by the Army Northern Command. Assault courses and trapeze in-flight swing training structures were also incorporated. After pre-jump training, recruits would speed-march 50 miles to Ringway to join the parachute course there. A barrage balloon was installed in November for refresher training, and in December the Second and Third Parachute battalions were also formed at Hardwick as well as the Number One Air Troop Royal Engineers and Skeleton Signals Squadron.

Chatsworth House, c1940s.

HARDWICK HALL. DERBYSHIRE

Hardwick Hall.

After the war ended the military accommodation was used by miners until 1959 when the camp was demolished and the site finally reinstated.

On 17 June 1940 the worst recorded disaster in British maritime history occurred. The *Lancastria,* a troop ship which was also carrying passengers, was bombed by the Germans near Saint-Nazaire. It sank in just twenty minutes and 4,000 people lost their lives; more than the *Titanic* and *Lusitania* put together, and twice as many as were lost from Sir Cloudesley Shovell's fleet of ships off the Isles of Scilly in 1707, Britain's worst sea disaster before the *Lancastria.* Although more than 2,000 people survived, over 30 of those who died came from the Glossop and Hadfield area in the north-west of Derbyshire. The tragedy hit the town hard and was a factor in Glossop helping to raise over £230,000 (£10,400,000) during the Warship Week of 1941. In July the Battle of Britain began and continued until the end of October. Britain won control of the skies but at a terrible cost.

It was quickly realised that air-raid shelters built at ground level did not offer much protection in the Second World War and that it was safer to be underground. In the Spanish civil war Barcelona, which had become a Republican (freedom fighters) stronghold, suffered heavy bombing from the Germans and the Italians. The city suffered 194 aerial attacks which destroyed 1,500 buildings and killed 2,500 people. The Spanish people have a very creative streak in their imaginations and it was in Barcelona that the first underground bomb-proof shelters were built. These initial shelters were built as a network of tunnels cut into the native bedrock. They were fitted with benches, toilets, electric lighting run from batteries, and first aid equipment. Several British engineers visited Barcelona to study the effects of bombing and the construction of the underground shelters. One, a scientist named J.B.S. Haldane, wrote:

> *There were four entrances which led down by ramps with a few steps to the tunnels. The ramps twisted repeatedly, until a depth of about 55 feet below the ground was reached. Here began a labyrinth of passages about 7 feet high by 4 feet broad. They were cut in the very tough soil of the district, and had no lining, and I think no supports such as pit props. They were, however, being lined with tiles with a cement backing so as to give a semi-circular arch and vertical walls.*

The idea of using tunnels as air-raid shelters caught on quickly after the commencement of hostilities. However, they were not within the reach of everyone and the idea of more simple and economic underground shelters evolved. Stanton Ironworks in Ilkeston manufactured Stanton shelters, consisting of segmented concrete parts which could be bolted together, partially buried, and supported on either side by banked earth, although these tended to be mostly used by the aviation industry. One of the most popular shelters was the Anderson shelter, named after its designer, Sir John Anderson. These measured 6ft 6ins (1.95m) by 4ft 6ins (1.35m) and were made from six curved and corrugated iron sheets bolted together which were then half buried in the earth in people's gardens. The entrance would be protected by 'a steel shield and an earthen blast wall'. However, Derbyshire was a mainly rural county with few towns to attract the German bombers. Remote farms and scattered hamlets scarcely bothered, preferring to shelter under the stairs or a table; in the larger villages some folk had an Anderson shelter. The alternative was the Morrison shelter, designed by John Baker and named after the Home Secretary of the day, Herbert Morrison. This was rather like a big steel dog cage measuring 6ft (2m) long by 4ft (1.2m) wide by 2ft 6ins (.75m) high. It was placed in a downstairs room, often the kitchen, where the top could be used as a table. A mattress was usually put inside for comfort and people sheltered there during raids since it could supposedly withstand tons of falling rubble. Some houses had basements and cellars, although it rapidly became obvious as the war progressed that deeper underground shelters were usually the most effective (like the sandstone tunnels at Underbank in neighbouring Stockport). Derby, Chesterfield, Glossop and Buxton, towns which had a larger population, had some public shelters. On the edge of Tupton, near Chesterfield, Monkey's Hollow in the local woods formerly housed a shelter for those employed at the nearby Clay Cross Works. Rolls Royce had their own air-raid shelters in Derby; so too did Stanton Gate Foundry near Ilkeston and factories in Chesterfield. Most town halls had subterranean basements, local churches had vaults, and there were canal tunnels (used and disused) which would also offer shelter. Glossop, for example, boasted of having no

Anderson or Morrison shelters at all, but there was a bunker, built of concrete with seats and electric light, which could house 200–300 people underneath the present telephone exchange; and a shelter in nearby Harehills Park beneath what is now the site of children's swings. In addition, there was a stone shelter with a sloping roof on King Street near Collier Brow and a brick shelter with steel doors and a flat roof on Shivering Row off Victoria Street,

ARP warden gas-protection clothing. (Courtesy of Manchester Central Library Local Studies)

which both lay on the southern side of the town in the Whitfield area. Shelters were built by Middletons at Woolley Bridge, and most schools and factories had their own shelters.

In June the national Labour Party had held a conference which expressed discontent with the way the war was being managed and extreme concern over the lack of air raid precautions (ARP) for ordinary working people and there was wide support for the idea of a Peoples' Vigilance Committee (PVC). Derby Labour Party followed this up with their own conference on Labour and the war and then, at the end of September, by the 'War Profits and Big Business' a result of bitter memories at how ordinary folk had suffered from profiteering in the Great War. There was also considerable support from both these conferences for a PVC. Although this had particular support from the Derby branch of NUDAW, many of those who supported the idea of a PVC were expelled from the Labour Party on the grounds it was a Communist idea and the Derby Railway Workshops TGWU members then decided that the whole concept of a PVC was being led by expelled Labour Party members. It really was, as some remarked at the time, a case of 'trouble at t' mill'.

The Blitzkrieg on English towns and cities just before Christmas in 1940 caught many unawares and 24,000 civilians were killed throughout the country. There was no knowing when or where the German bombers would strike next, so large numbers of city people chose to spend their Christmas in air-raid shelters and there was a sudden demand for small or short Christmas trees which would fit into the shelters. Derbyshire had mostly escaped the horrors of the Blitz as, with the exception of Derby and Chesterfield, there really wasn't much to attract the attention of the Luftwaffe because they didn't know about Harpur Hill in Buxton or the secret naval installation in Glossop. Nevertheless, the village of Youlgreave sustained a hit on 23 December, the first night of the Blitz on Manchester. It was muttered darkly that the Luftwaffe were after the DB Battery company in Bakewell which manufactured batteries for submarines. Rumours had it that dozens of incendiary bombs fell although little damage was done and it was probably caused by bombs being jettisoned after the Manchester attack by German planes anxious to escape and return home. The Luftwaffe had bigger fish than Youlgreave to fry and were focussed on the northern industrial cities such as Manchester, Sheffield, and Liverpool.

By this time, 41,000 British troops had been captured on the Continent and this affected many Derbyshire families. The mood was generally sombre and there was little heart for Christmas cheer; the children looked forward to it as the one festive occasion they were still permitted to enjoy. Easter had been cancelled this year as well as Guy Fawkes celebrations. There had been church services, but eggs were rationed and chocolate was practically non-existent. There had been no boiled eggs to face paint for breakfast on Easter Day and no sweet treats to munch through afterwards. Instead the

Remains of a Second World War pillbox on Harpur Hill, Buxton.

government had promoted raw carrots on sticks to replace sweets and ice cream as there was a surplus of carrots and the government decided this would encourage healthy eating. Younger children born at the beginning of the war would not taste ice cream until the early 1950s. Christmas spending nose-dived, but £10 million (just under £500,000,000) of war bonds were bought nationwide in the week before Christmas. In Derbyshire, both holly and mistletoe grow wild, and many houses were decorated with greenery as was still the custom at Hallowe'en. Most presents were homemade and many were simply for the children. Small dolls' houses, toy soldiers, or model ships made from bits of wood, or knitted dolls and teddy bears, were favourites; the most popular present for adults was a bar of soap. Scant rations of ham, bacon, suet, butter and margarine were saved for the main meal and home-grown vegetables (in season British vegetables would include mainly potatoes, parsnips, onions, cabbage, kale and sprouts) and homemade pickles or chutneys would accompany Christmas dinner. Puddings were made without fruit, nuts or marzipan. Alcohol and nuts were prohibitively expensive. Cheese was strictly rationed. Apples and pears were the only British fruits in season and these were scarce. There were, however, extra rations of tea and sugar in the week before Christmas. Again, in rural Derbyshire, there was always something to be had from the countryside, such as rabbits, pigeons, wild herbs, and whinberries (plentiful in the county during the summer months and preserved or bottled by Derbyshire housewives).

Any form of travel was discouraged. This was partly due to petrol rationing and partly due to the need to keep the roads and railways available for the transportation of troops and war supplies. The BBC did their best to add a little gaiety to proceedings, broadcasting variety shows, the King's Speech, a programme called *Kitchen Front* (broadcast daily at 8 am involving issues of rationing, use of available foods, trying new wartime recipes, discouraging food waste etc.) and a sermon from the cathedral ruins in Coventry. Christmas church services continued as normal, but bells could not be rung (as this would signify invasion) and windows could not be lit up. Cinema celebrated Christmas with the release of *The Great Dictator* starring Charlie Chaplin, a film which poked satirical fun at Hitler. In one scene, Chaplin, dressed as Hitler, his hair and moustache an absolute 'brilliantined' copy, shinned up a floor-to-ceiling curtain, clutching a small globe, and announced to his startled lieutenants below 'I want to be alone!' Hitler was beyond furious when he learned of the film and it is rumoured that Charlie Chaplin was at the top of his blacklist for when, as he believed, he would conquer England.

CHAPTER THREE

1941

Hitler's policy of Blitzkrieg, German for 'lightning war', was based on speed, surprise, coordination and rapid mass attacks on an area to cause maximum destruction, damage to infrastructure, chaos and panic. In mid-December 1940 Sheffield suffered badly from the German Blitzkrieg which killed 600 people, injured 1,500, destroyed 3,000 homes and damaged the steel works. Manchester suffered in similar fashion just before Christmas that year. The casualties in Manchester were lower in number than Sheffield, but so much of the city was set ablaze that the Germans believed that they had almost entirely destroyed it. Although neither of these cities are in Derbyshire, both have borders with the county. Consequently, in order to try and protect Manchester and Sheffield from further attacks a decision was taken to build decoy sites, known as 'Starfish sites', in remote places on the Derbyshire moors. RAF Balloon Command were in charge of the Starfish sites. These decoy targets were intended to confuse German bombers into thinking they were bombing a city when, in fact, they were bombing empty countryside. Each Starfish site (or Special Fire site from which they took their name) had an air-raid shelter for the operational crew and several different devices to simulate lights and fire. The sites were usually built between 4 miles (7km) and 10 miles (17km) from the place they were intended to protect and at least 1 mile (1.75km) from any village or settlement. Vehicle tracks could be faked by spraying pesticide onto surrounding grass and heather. Glow boxes simulated city lights. 'Fire baskets' on stands about 20ft (6m) tall contained fires of creosote or coal onto which petrol or diesel was dripped from overhead tanks to simulate exploding incendiary bombs hitting buildings after the attacking planes had passed over. Up to 30 tons of fuel could be stored on site for this purpose. Water was then pumped onto the fires giving clouds of steam which looked like smoke. The 'lights' and 'fires' were controlled from concrete bunkers.

This project was an extension of a decoy programme designed to protect airfields and factories devised by Colonel John Turner, and there were a number of starfish sites within the area of the south-western Pennines. Starfish bombing decoy SF9G was one of nine 'starfish' decoy sites protecting Manchester. It

Remains of the starfish site at Curbar near the Yorkshire border.

was situated up on Ludworth Moor, a lonely stretch of moorland close to Glossop in Derbyshire. Although it remained in use for most of the war, the land was subsequently given over to agricultural purposes and today no trace of it remains. Sheffield had a number of Starfish sites surrounding the city, of which three were in Derbyshire. Starfish bombing decoy SF3D was at Norton, close to the Derbyshire/Yorkshire boundary near Eccleshall. It was in use until 1943 but no features of it remain and the land is now in agricultural use. Eckington, midway between Chesterfield and Sheffield, was home to C10D, a civil bombing decoy designed to protect the London-Midland-Scottish railway. It was in use 1942–1943 but, again, nothing survives of this feature. Possibly the best known of the Derbyshire sites protecting Sheffield was on the Curbar moors, near Baslow and Culver, and about 12 miles from Sheffield. Curbar is a pretty village in the Derbyshire Dales and the local Calver, Curbar and Froggatt historical society have painstakingly recorded numerous details of the site. Starfish bombing decoy SF3A was in use from 1940 until possibly as late as 1944, but again no features have survived above ground although there are clear indications of foundation debris and shallow ditches. The land, like the other sites, is now being used for agricultural purposes but there are marked footpaths across the area. The site is remote, wild and windswept and, on the ground, it is hard to believe its proximity to Sheffield. Stanage Edge and Burbage Moor nearby were also the sites of other decoys of which no traces remain, largely obliterated by exposure to the elements at altitude. Ironically, Starfish bombing decoy SF4A was commissioned late in 1940 at Ticknall to deflect the bombing of Derby, but it failed to protect the Rolls Royce factory in Derby from being bombed in 1942. This decoy was operational until 1944 although there are no features remaining save for a curved trackway. Other decoys included Starfish bombing decoy SF4B at Long Whatton and Diseworth, near the junction of the A42 and the M1, designed to protect the railway marshalling yards at Toton and the Rolls Royce factory in Osmaston; and Starfish bombing decoy SF4C at Swarkestone, close to the present A50, which was intended to protect the Qualcast Works and the city of Derby. Both these latter sites were operational until 1943–1944 but today no trace remains of them, the former buried firmly under the M1 motorway, the latter reverted to farmland. In addition, there was Civil Bombing Decoy site C17B at Ambaston/Thulston, two small hamlets which are part of Elvaston parish, adjacent to the Derby Southern Bypass. The aim of this decoy was to deflect bombers from the Chaddesden marshalling yards. It was mainly active from 1941–1943 but no trace of it remains today.

The village of Tupton was never intended as a decoy site but that is what it inadvertently became on 15 March 1941. Tupton is 4 miles from Chesterfield, 8 miles from Barrow Hill and 1 mile from the industrial area of Clay Cross. The Luftwaffe were determined to bomb the Tube Works in Chesterfield as well as the railway junction at Horns Bridge and nearby Barrow Hill. Chesterfield

Model of soldier saluting fallen comrades at the Primary School in Tupton.

and its surrounds, however, had excellent black-out facilities and the German planes became confused and disorientated as to where they should drop their bombs. However, their presence had been noted on the ground and had drawn searchlights and anti-aircraft fire. One pilot of a German aircraft now fleeing Chesterfield decided to drop his bombs at random. They hit Ward Street in the village of Tupton, demolishing a row of houses and killing eleven people. The war memorial outside St John's Church records the names of those who were lost, and in the grounds of the village primary school opposite the church there is a wire replica of a saluting soldier with a poppy pinned to his chest. The actual site of the bombing on Ward Street has been commemorated by the establishment of the Community Gardens, an area of two circular cobbled areas surrounded by seats, greenery and flower beds, where there is a great sense of peace, in contrast to the absolute terror which the inhabitants must have felt on that March night in 1941.

Chesterfield was bombed again in an effort to destroy manufacturing enterprises and lines of transport, but the town emerged from the Blitz relatively unscathed due to its stringent black-out precautions. It had become a place of interest to the Luftwaffe being one of Derbyshire's few centres of industry, and the targets of most interest were Horns Bridge, Bryan Donkin's factory, and local engineering works. The Tube Works produced thousands of hydrogen cylinders for the defensive barrage balloons in 1939 and then switched to cylinder production for all the armed forces including oxygen cylinders for aircraft and submarine crews, fire-fighting and rescue equipment, casings for bombs, shells, sten guns and mortar barrels. Bryan Donkin's factory specialised in manufacturing compressors. Chesterfield was also

St John's and war memorial, Tupton.

situated on a large coal field and there were a number of coal mines in the area and an extensive railway network with important junctions at Horns Bridge and Barrow Hill. Horns Bridge carried three major railway lines: the Great Western, the LNER, and the Midland. Barrow Hill serviced engines, trucks and carriages from these railway companies, and also had a 'roundhouse', a large working turntable encircled with twenty-four tracks, thereby enabling ease of turning rolling stock around. In the event the Luftwaffe miscalculated again and the German bombs hit a golf course a few miles away. Alfreton and Somercotes in the Amber Valley also became targets when the Luftwaffe dropped large numbers of incendiary bombs on their way to bomb Sheffield and jettisoned remaining bombs after a raid on the city. The Sheffield railway line passed through Alfreton and the German bombers followed the line, although often mistaking their targets in the black-out. Most of the bombs fell on fields so there were few casualties and little damage.

Glossop and Buxton in the north-west of the county also escaped the attentions of the Luftwaffe at this time, mainly because the Germans had no idea that they were of much importance. Secrecy had been absolute. Buxton had the largest store of ammunition in the country stashed safely in underground tunnels built through Harpur Hill. Careful camouflage during construction had given the appearance of just a few quarry workings in the countryside just outside Buxton. In the centre of Glossop an old mill which had stood empty for twelve years, unnoticed within the complex of mills in which it stood, became a top-secret factory and storage depot for highly sensitive radio equipment used by the Royal Navy. For this reason it was known locally as the 'Admiralty'. A Signals School stood in former buildings on what is now the car park, this was also top-secret and was surrounded by wire fencing and security guards. The former Lux Lux factory in Howard Town Mill was home to radio specialists during the war who serviced radio sets and handled complicated radar systems. In the neighbouring village of Padfield, Maconochie's, who manufactured Spam, Pan Yan pickle, and the tinned meat and vegetable stew used by the troops in the Great War, as well as several other foodstuffs, quietly slipped into the Waterside Mill complex having been bombed out during the London blitz. Other mills close by produced fabrics for parachutes and barrage balloons, and the 'top mill' was said to house a rations store.

Despite all the problems caused by the idea of Peoples' Vigilance Committees, a PVC convention had taken place in mid-January. The Sheffield, Derbyshire and Nottinghamshire area sent ninety-five delegates. This convention demanded a 'Peoples' Government and a People's Peace.' This sparked immediate concern, especially among Derbyshire TGWU members, that the whole thing was simply a Communist plot. This led to the government taking various measures and the *Daily Worker*, the only newspaper to actively support the idea of a PVC, was suppressed for nearly two years. Protests about communism, however, became much more muted when Russia joined the war on the side of the Allies in June 1941 after Hitler made his ill-fated decision to invade Russian territory. Many trades unionists were mollified by Ernest Bevin, the general secretary of the TGWU being appointed minister of labour, although it turned into a double-edged sword as the government increasingly took over control of labour, deciding where workers should be allocated, and began the practice of applying Essential Work Orders (EWOs). These forbade workers in essential industries, 'scheduled undertakings', to leave without express permission and heavy fines were imposed for being either absent from work or consistently late. An unfortunate Derby lad was fined £15 (£678) for being regularly late for work. The local NUDAW secretary was transferred to Rolls Royce to work on munitions and twenty-seven men from Derby Corporation were sent to work on repairing damage from the Blitz in London. In return, minimum wages were guaranteed and employers had to recognise employment terms and conditions, on the condition that no action by workers should be taken until at least three weeks after the initial reports of grievances and intentions to strike. Disputes were to be settled by arbitration. This benefitted transport workers, engineering workers and South Derbyshire miners in particular, all of whom gained decent wage increases. In addition, positively involving workers in greater participation was found to help the war effort in general. The Derby TGWU weren't quite so keen to help foreign workers. There was still a deep-seated suspicion of foreigners. Refugees were arriving in Britain keen to help the war effort by working. Salton's of Ashbourne employed a number of Czech workers, two of whom eventually became members of the local TGWU committee, and the TGWU applied for war bonuses for all the Czech workers, despite being wary of possible communists.

The government reminded folk of the importance of civil defence, and of the need to remember the demands on shipping and to be as economical as possible. It was recommended that luxury goods should be restricted, woollen clothing should be left for military rather than civilian use, and consumption of bacon and sugar should be reduced. The space taken up on ships by these items could then be redeployed for cargoes of iron or machine tools. Thanks to the phoney war and the lack of action on land the government felt many people had failed to realise the immediate severity of the threat that was facing the country. People were more concerned with the day-to-day business of living, of paying increased taxation, and of coping with rising prices and the cost of living. The problem of the black market and profiteers had already been recognised at government level and the Prices of Goods Bill had been passed to curtail, if not completely abolish, the mean and miserable practice of making a mint of money by withholding supplies until prices were forced up. Food rationing was in full force and there were inevitable food queues. Imports of alcohol ceased in October and reduced supplies of sugar and barley meant that there were shortages of beer and whisky; there was also a shortage of petrol.

The Limitation of Supplies (Cloth and Apparel) Order was passed and civilian clothing was rationed for the first time at the beginning of June. This was in an effort both to conserve raw materials and to free up workers and manufactories for the production of items necessary for the war, especially munitions. Purchases of all types of clothing for everyone were subject to ration coupons in the same way as food. It was hard to keep up with fashions or growing children. The Board of Trade sponsored several ranges of 'utility clothing' which had strict specifications on the amounts of material to be used and the labour involved. No turn-ups were allowed on trousers, nor were double-breasted suits allowed. Skirt and coat lengths were regulated. All utility clothing carried a label stating 'CC41' which stood for 'Controlled Commodity', and '41' referred to the year that this measure had been instigated. Leading fashion designers, like Norman Hartnell and Hardy Amies, were commissioned to design clothing for the utility ranges and maximum prices chargeable for both cloth and clothing were laid down. Women became adept at 'make do and mend' by using old clothes and curtains to make new items of wear or by adorning faded clothes with bits of lace or ribbon. Some items such as silk or nylon stockings were difficult, if not impossible, to obtain and many girls and women either wore ankle socks or nothing with their shoes. The armed forces and school uniforms relied on thick lisle stockings which were simply for regulation purposes and, in winter, warmth but they were not popular. Most nylon stockings still had vertical seams along their backs and those wanting to dress up and look chic emulated these stocking seams by drawing them down their legs with eyeliner pencils or charcoal. Lines of 'national footwear' were also produced although the height of heels was strictly limited. Women became very adept at making clothes for themselves and their families. Rationing and utility regulations might govern commercial supplies of clothing, but no-one could tell a housewife what to do with a pair of her old curtains or a dress that she would never wear again. Anything made from textile materials could be utilised for something else. 'Hand-me-downs' became a well-used, if disliked, phrase among children, clothes made or obtained for a first child would be handed down to siblings. Hems would be taken up and down, waistbands would be taken in…or out. Trousers would be lengthened or shortened. Coat and dress seams would be altered. One Sawley (near Long Eaton) father cut strips from an old bicycle tyre so that he could mend the holes in his children's shoes. The system of hand-me-downs seemed to be particularly hard for teenage girls and young women who simply longed for something new of their own to wear. Sons and daughters would scoff as they watched their mother or father saving every little thing, like bits of string, pieces of paper, elastic bands, scraps of material etc., that they thought might come in useful one day, but they often found themselves grateful for their parents' forethought and thrift.

Thrift and economy were also key words for wartime weddings. One of the major reasons for people choosing to marry in wartime was that the groom was due to be sent to fight overseas. White weddings were often considered inappropriate because of the material resources needed for the bride's dress and those of the bridesmaids. Old or spare parachute silk was keenly sought, but a bride was considered fortunate indeed if she managed to obtain any. Those who did wear long white dresses had either borrowed heirlooms from family or friends or had managed to find a second-hand one for sale. Many brides wore a two-piece knee-length suit, which could be used on other occasions, or made themselves a simple dress which could be used for everyday wear afterwards. Bouquet flowers were often picked from gardens or fields. Film was scarce and a bride considered herself lucky if she got even a couple of photographs of her wedding. There was usually no formal meal or party; and if there was it might be no more than a tray of oven-baked sausages. Rations were pooled to make a wedding cake, each guest received a slice with a cup of tea after the ceremony prior to the bride and groom leaving for the short time they would have together before being separated by the needs of the war. One Derbyshire bride who married in the summer thought herself blessed to be given a two-tier wedding cake after her mother had begged rations from all her friends. She shared the bottom tier with her wedding guests and wrapped the top tier to be stored in a tin for Christmas. However, the 'marzipan' on the cake had been made with soya flour and when she opened the tin on Christmas day to share her treasure as a Christmas treat she found the cake to be completely inedible.

A week before Christmas the British government passed the National Service (No.2) Act. All men and women aged 18–60 were now liable for national service which included military service for those under the age of 51. It was the first time women had been conscripted and also the first military registration of those aged 18 years old. It also raised the question of conscientious objectors once more. The legislation had made provision for folk to object to fighting on moral grounds. There were nearly four times as many conscientious objectors as during the Great War; and there was a register of conscientious objectors containing around 6,000 names of which a third were women. The whole question of conscientious objectors was a difficult one. During the Second World War there were three main grounds which were religious, moral and political; most objectors fell into the first two categories. There was a three-tier system for objectors: they could be registered unconditionally; registered as willing to do civilian work essential to the war effort, or registered to carry out non-combatant duties in the army. The reaction to conscientious objectors was roughly the same as in the Great War, with many people still labelling them as cowards and many employers refusing to give them jobs. They came from all walks of life and all strata of society. Many of the conscientious objectors simply said that they could not take human life but most were willing to work in non-combatant roles. This was accepted and numbers of them were sent to the battle fronts where they worked as medical orderlies, drivers, auxiliaries, dispatch riders, mechanics, clerks, essential war work occupations such as mining, agriculture, forestry or hospitals. The main problems were caused by those who refused to contribute in any way. Fenner Brockway, a leading conscientious objector during the Great War, said during the Second World War that 'the conscientious objector has no right to reject war in the present unless he spends his life in helping to make a future without war.' Local military tribunals were set up before which conscientious objectors pleaded their case, and rejections of objectors' claims varied between 6 per cent and 41 per cent. The arguments before and against remained the same as during the Great War. On the one hand people felt that they had the right to choose whether to fight or not and the freedom to follow their moral conscience, whilst on the other hand, especially with an adversary like Hitler, it was absolutely necessary for others to fight, and perhaps to die, in order for them to have that freedom of choice. 'There are some wars that just have to be fought,' said one Derbyshire lady sadly; and a tribunal chairman, on hearing a pacifist's objection to fighting turned and said 'Even God is not a pacifist for He kills us all in the end.' As well as military conscription there was also what was termed 'industrial conscription'. From May 1940 onwards the Minister of Labour and National Service had the authority to 'direct any person to perform such services which in the opinion of the Minister the person directed is capable of performing'. This was so that essential industries such as food provision, armaments, munitions, shipbuilding, aircraft manufacturers, for example, would not suffer from labour shortages and be unable to fulfil their obligations. Also included were compulsory fire watching duties. Tribunals had scant patience with objectors to industrial conscription and there were several imprisonments. Some conscientious objectors maintained that although they would always help fellow beings in distress, they would not register for any rota that was part of the war effort. This kind of objection was usually summarily dismissed and those objecting were either fined or imprisoned. Rural Derbyshire, like other rural areas, experienced problems with some of the more extreme conscientious objectors who refused to help the war effort in any way and who, deprived of the opportunity to earn a living by their stance, were shunned by family and friends, and decided to live rough. They slept in barns or sheds, stealing food from farms where they could. In more remote locations farmers' wives and daughters might often be alone during the daytime and, although at little risk of attack from conscientious objectors, would be frightened at finding a strange man on their property. Initially they would not even know if he was English or German, friend or foe. Conscientious objectors at least willing to

Derwent Reservoir, Derwent Valley.

help with the war effort, although not in a combatant way, could often find temporary labouring jobs on farms because agricultural workers were in short supply, but they had to move on when the local authorities became aware of their presence. It was a difficult and often insoluble problem.

After the rash of aircraft crashes in the Dark Peak during the latter months of 1940, the year of 1941 had begun on a quieter note, but it was not to last. Wellington Mk/IC L7811/OJ-C was a member of 149 Squadron based at Mildenhall in Suffolk. The aircraft took part in a raid on Bremen (aiming to bomb the Mercedes Benz complex) during the night of 11/12 February. Before turning for home the plane had sustained damage from anti-aircraft fire and by the time it reached England the radio and several other instruments were not working. There was total cloud cover and the crew were unable to ascertain their position as the fuel tanks ran low. Eventually they were left with no option but to abandon the aircraft. All six crew landed safely near Haddon Hall, not far from Bakewell; while the plane flew on a further 2 or 3 miles before crashing into a hillside. A few weeks later, two aircraft, Master Mk.I T8324 and Master Mk.I N7870, were lost from the same Shropshire training squadron in the same area (around Bakewell and Hathersage) in consecutive nights at the end of March. In both cases poor weather was to blame. The pilot of T8324 was killed when his aircraft flew into a hillside; but the pilot of N7870 managed to crash-land and survived. Test flights and training flights could be hazardous over the Peak District at the best of times. Defiant Mk.I N1766 crashed in mid-April west of the Derwent Reservoir after radio failure and a fault developing in the Merlin engine. Both crew bailed out and survived but had to hike some considerable distance for help; one walking to the remote Alport Castles, the other to the Derwent valley. In late May, the pilot of another aircraft on a training flight was not quite so lucky when he became lost in rain and tried to crash-land near Tissington. He was injured and his aircraft, Oxford Mk.I N4641, was damaged although it was subsequently repaired and served until 1944. Two days later yet another training flight came to grief close to Ashbourne. Miles Magister Mk.I L6909 became engulfed in rain and cloud so the pilot decided that he and his pupil would force-land the aircraft and then take off again after the weather had cleared a bit. The landing was successful but take-off was up a slight hill and the aircraft was unable to gain sufficient speed before hitting a stone boundary wall. However, the crew were uninjured and the plane sustained only comparatively minor damage. There was another crash in the Ashbourne area in early December when Magister T9823 was on a test flight with a mission to collect spare parts from Wolverhampton and return to RAF Burnaston near Derby. The pilot lost his way in low cloud and poor visibility and flew into a hillside, he was killed but his passenger survived. July saw two fatal crashes close to Edale, Blenheim Mk.IV Z5870 was flying from Lincolnshire to Manchester with the pilot and three passengers on board, the area was blanketed in low cloud and the aircraft simply flew into Kinder Scout, killing everyone on board. The angle of the plane had determined the total destruction of the front half of the aircraft, which contained the pilot and passengers, although the rear half was relatively unscathed. On the last day of the month, Wellington Mk.IC W5719/JN-S was returning to Yorkshire after a bombing raid on Cologne when it became enveloped in low cloud, losing its way and flying into steep ground at Grindsbrook Clough. All the crew were killed with the exception of the rear gunner who was flung clear and survived. In late August another Miles Magister Mk.I, this time L6908, also on a training flight when the pilot became lost, crash-landed near Chapel-en-le-Frith, but hit a tree, injuring the pilot. Six days later Oxford Mk.I V3210 crashed in the same area. The pilot was flying solo on a training flight, flying above the cloud. When he tried to land and entered the cloud once more he flew straight into the moorland. Amazingly the pilot survived and was able to walk away from the aircraft. At the end of August Defiant Mk.I N3378 crashed when it flew into the northern side of Bleaklow, a remote and hostile area as its name suggests, of the north western Dark Peak. The aircraft appeared to have deviated from its more eastern flight path due to thunderstorms but encountered dense low cloud over the Pennines. Both people on board were killed. Two weeks before Christmas, Bleaklow claimed another victim. Botha Mk.I W5103 was flying from a factory near Leeds to Hawarden in Cheshire. The pilot flew above thick cloud, but at this time altimeters often malfunctioned and unable to see below he descended before he was clear of the hills. The aircraft simply flew into the ground and the pilot was killed. In mid-October Defiant MK.I T3921, on a night training exercise, crashed on Shining Tor near Buxton, injuring its crew of two. The reason does not appear to be known but the crew may have become disorientated in the dark and it is likely the weather would have been

War memorial St Michael and All Angels Church, Hathersage.

cloudy or wet at that time of year. A month later the pilot of a Spitfire, Mk.IIA P7560, on a training exercise from Shrewsbury, became disorientated due to bad weather and crashed near Harpur Hill in Buxton. The pilot, who survived uninjured, was clearly unaware of the huge munitions dump beneath the hill.

It seems incredible that so many crashes could occur in such a short period of time over such a comparatively small area but the Pennines have always been problematical for aircraft. Rapidly changing weather conditions, strong winds, thick mists, and the very nature of the terrain are treacherous. However, the geographical location, low density population and isolation of the Derbyshire Pennines made them popular as flight paths and grounds for military training exercises. Altimeters frequently malfunctioned, and often all the pilot had to guide him was his own skill and intuition. Even today, when aircraft have state-of-the-art technology, the flight paths above the Derbyshire hills are much higher than the flight paths which would have been taken by the smaller and less advanced Second World War planes.

By December 1941 Christmas was what's known as 'on the ration'. Wrapping paper was extremely scarce and it was hard to keep Christmas presents a surprise. Food rationing was becoming much stricter with decreased allocations of cheese, jam (including mincemeat), milk and eggs. From the beginning of December everyone also received a monthly allocation of sixteen points for various foodstuffs. This was not overly generous and 1lb (0.5kg) of luncheon meat or 1.5lbs (0.75kg) of tinned salmon could cost a whole month's points. Tinned salmon was a great favourite for Sunday tea in many northern homes. Most foodstuffs, alcohol and cigarettes were now in short supply. The Ministry of Food, attempting to keep up spirits, issued the type of message that could only come from a government department: 'no gay bowls of fruit, vegetables have such jolly colours. The cheerful glow of the carrots, the rich crimson of the beetroot, and the emerald of parsley – it looks as delightful as it tastes.' The good folk of Derbyshire simply shrugged their shoulders with a wry smile and wondered if the writer of this message had any understanding of real life before making do as best they could for Christmas dinner. However, after the bombing of Pearl Harbour on 7 December the United States had now entered the war on the side of the Allies and Britain no longer felt so alone.

CHAPTER FOUR

1942

In January 1942 the 1/5th Battalion of the Sherwood Foresters was sent to Singapore, arriving shortly before it fell to the Japanese. Subsequently, they were captured by the Japanese and made to work on the Burma-Siam railway. They were very badly treated and a total of 450 men died as a result. The Battalion was severely depleted by this, having already lost men to German captivity from fighting with the BEF prior to and during the Dunkerque evacuations. A further blow to the Foresters was when the 1st Battalion were ordered to surrender at Tobruk early in 1942. It was in the summer of 1942 that El Alamein, a small Egyptian town and railway halt on the Mediterranean coast, entered the general consciousness of the British public. The First Battle of El Alamein (1–27 July) had been fought in Egypt between the Afrika Corps of the Axis forces commanded by Field Marshal Rommel (the Desert Fox) and the Eighth Army of the Allied forces commanded by General Auchinleck. The Axis forces were coming dangerously close to the cities and ports of Egypt, although the Allies had so far managed to prevent further advances. The Second Battle of El Alamein (23 October–11 November) took place with Lieutenant General Bernard Montgomery ('Monty' as he became affectionately known) replacing General Auchinleck as commander of the Allied Forces. The 14th Battalion of the Sherwood Foresters acquitted itself with distinction at the Second Battle of El Alamein in November 1942 in which the 2nd Derbyshire Yeomanry also fought valiantly. Monty's victory at El Alamein was a turning point in the war. The resulting victory for the Allies ended the Axis threat to Egypt and the Suez Canal as well as to the Persian and Middle Eastern oilfields and marked a turning point in the North Africa campaign.

By 1942 the local Derbyshire authorities had decided that there was a distinct need to train cadets for community service. To this end the Girls Training Corps Company 646 had been set up and were based at Somercotes Infants School. The Air Ministry had Air Training Corps for boys below military age in various parts of the county. The First North Derbyshire Squadron was formed in Buxton and drilled on the Ferodo carpark in Chapel-en-le-Frith. In Glossop the Royal Observer Corps (Charlie Group) manned an underground bunker and observation post for spotting planes on Taylor's Hill near Pyegrove Fields. Those working there during the war described it as a dark, rather damp and cheerless place. The bunker still exists, although internally it is not in a good state and is only visible as a small earth-covered hummock on which local cows appear to find the grass rather tasty. The Home Guard (more popularly known as 'Dad's Army') played an important role as well. They guarded the water supplies in the reservoirs; manned outposts high up on the moors keeping a look-out for paratroopers; and they also performed a number of community services as and when required. Regular drills were important and these took place in schools, town halls and church halls. Men who were either too young or too old, or suffered from medical problems, made up most members of the Home Guard. Initially they were given khaki armbands printed with 'LDV' (Local Defence Volunteers) and later were supplied with a uniform. By day they had full-time jobs, mostly related to the war effort, and in the evenings they drilled in local halls. Night-time watches were rostered to watch for enemy action of any type and to reassure civilians by their presence. The towns and villages, railways and reservoirs of Derbyshire were guarded in this way, but it was impossible to cover all the many isolated farmsteads. However, most farmers had a gun and knew how to use it.

Although the well-known television series, Dad's Army, gently poked fun at the Home Guard, they were in fact the first line of defence if the Germans invaded. They received sufficient training to track the enemy and to attempt to keep the enemy at bay until regular military forces could arrive to deal with them. In the event the Derbyshire Home Guard were not needed for general defence purposes although they did assist in capturing German aircrew who bailed out of damaged planes over Derbyshire. Coastal platoons of the Home Guard also guarded Britain's shores to prevent the Germans landing by stealth, but Derbyshire is a landlocked county where the danger came from the air.

More importantly, in 1942 it was decided to build additional operational and training airfields in the more southern parts of the county. The Dark Peak in the north-west of the county was unsuitable, and the White Peak around Buxton and Castleton was very hilly terrain some of which was unstable. Bad weather often affected both areas. Derby, the most obvious and vulnerable target for the German bombers, had its own airfield at RAF Burnaston. (Burnaston closed in 1990, and the site now lies beneath a car factory. The present Derby airfield is a couple of miles away and has only been operational since the 1990s.) Before the war RAF Burnaston had run air-training schools for which Tiger Moths and Miles Magisters were used. During the war the Air Schools were used to train RAF Volunteer Reserve pilots. Miles Magisters began to supersede Tiger Moths and a number of them were 'kept in full flying trim' at the airfield. As the war progressed Hurricanes and Spitfires, as well as Lancasters and Vickers Wellingtons, superseded the Miles Magisters in turn. Darley Moor airfield, a couple of miles south of Ashbourne, was built in 1942 although it wasn't actually opened until 1943. This airfield was used for training purposes as well by Number 42 Operational Training Unit of the RAF, in similar aircraft to those used at RAF Burnaston. The RAF also built several concrete runways, most of which are now converted into Darley Moor Racetrack. RAF Ashbourne was larger and had three paved runways, hard standings for the planes, four hangars and a control tower, as well as assorted outbuildings for maintenance purposes. Construction had begun late in 1941 and was completed in 1942. It was intended as a base for Vickers Wellington aircraft but also had Armstrong Whitworth and Bristol Blenheim planes. However, the altitude of Ashbourne and frequent bad weather caused the airfield to be relegated to a training base alongside RAF Darley Moor. It was used by three units: Number 42 Operational Training Unit; Number 81 Operational Training Unit; and Number 28 Maintenance Unit (the same unit who were responsible for the ammunitions stores at Harpur Hill). RAF Church Broughton, about 14 miles to the east of Derby, was a more cosmopolitan enterprise. It was a 'satellite airfield' for Number 27 Operational Training Unit and it was used by Wellington Bombers, Lancasters, Liberators, Handley Page Halifax aircraft, B-17 Flying Fortresses, and Spitfires. The airfield boasted three runways, two hangars, a watch tower, and numerous small huts and outbuildings. Later in the war, in 1944, RAF Church Broughton would be used by Rolls Royce for secret testing of early jet engines. Personnel included Englishmen, Australians, New Zealanders, Americans, Canadians, Czechs and Poles, many of whom lost their lives in action. At nearby Sudbury what is now HMP Sudbury was then an American hospital and visitors often arrived via RAF Church Broughton.

The life expectancy of many pilots was tragically short. In RAF Bomber Command the death rate was almost one in two. The average age of bomber crew members was 22 and their life expectancy in combat was roughly four weeks; only two weeks for a rear or tail gunner. Twenty-five missions had to be completed before a crew could be given home leave. The stress was enormous and several cracked under the strain. This problem was recognised by RAF commanders and Rockside Hall in Wellington Street, Matlock was taken over by the RAF and converted into a hospital to treat 'battle fatigued aircrew'. A patient could be admitted simply on the grounds that they had refused to fly on a mission because it was an indication their stress levels could be a danger to themselves and to their fellow crew members.

The plane crashes of the Derbyshire Dark and White Peaks continued but diminished in number, although there were several instances of plane crashes in and around the Cheshire, Yorkshire and Staffordshire moorlands. Those, however, are not within the scope of this book. There was a real tragedy in late January when Handley Page Hampden Mk.I AE381 was sent on a training flight from RAF Skellingthorpe near Lincoln. It was a night-time navigation exercise which took place in a heavy blizzard. Becoming disorientated and unable to see anything, or to find their way home, the crew radioed Ringway Airport in Manchester for help and permission to land there. The pilot was told to make a 180 degree turn and head for the airfield but before he could do so the plane flew straight into the western edge of Kinder Scout and burst into flames, all four crew members died instantly. The modern idiom 'lessons will be learned' may well have applied, as in the first half of 1942 there were almost no crash incidents recorded in Derbyshire, except the forced landing of Westland Lysander Mk.IIIA V9729 at Cronkstone, near Buxton at the end of May, when it had simply run out of fuel. The plane was little damaged and the crew were unhurt. It was mid-October before another real tragedy occurred, when Avro Anson Mk.I L7968 was on 'night navigation' exercise but the crew mistook the position of one of the navigation beacons. Consequently, when the aircraft came in to land on what they believed was the airfield it flew straight into a hillside instead, killing all four crew.

Derby itself had managed to escape the main ravages of the Blitz, but on 27 July 1942 a single German plane, a Junkers Ju88 under low cloud cover, launched an unexpected attack on the city and just before 8 am hit the Rolls Royce factory. Rolls Royce, launched in Manchester in 1904, had its main manufacturing complex at Osmaston, a suburb of Derby, from 1980–2007. The Nightingale Works, which were the main works, manufactured the famous Rolls Royce 'Silver Ghost' cars; but during the Second World War

VALENTINE'S "AIRCRAFT RECOGNITION" CARDS

VALENTINE & SONS, LTD.,
DUNDEE and LONDON.
Printed in Gt. Britain.

Junkers aircraft which carried out several aerial attacks on Derbyshire in the Second World War.

most of the complex was given over by the spring of 1940 to the manufacture of Merlin engines, which were vital for the Spitfire and Hurricane fighter planes and for cargo aircraft. The Junkers plane flew low over the factory dropping four bombs which hit the central stores and a few houses opposite, before turning and strafing civilians in the area and shooting down a barrage balloon. Twenty-three people were killed, twelve of them within the factory. One-hundred-and-twenty people were injured, some seriously, and the factory was badly damaged.

At the other end of the county New Mills, Rowarth and Hayfield had been bombed in early July. Although the two German Ju 88 bombers did not hit their intended target, which had been the de Havilland factory at Lostock near Bolton, they left a trail of havoc and destruction. They had conceived a clever plan of flying low so that they were beneath radar detection, but they had not allowed for the low cloud which so often affects coastal and Pennine areas. Unable to see where they were, the Germans crossed the coast further south than they had realised and then became disorientated when trying to assess their location on their maps. Unable to locate their target they did not drop their bombs despite passing close to the Trafford Park industrial complex. They were still flying very low and very fast but had begun to be concerned about their fuel supply for getting back to their base and decided to jettison their bombs. As they flew over New Mills town centre one plane dropped bombs near the Mousley Bottom gas works and on Torrs Gorge near Lowes Mill (now Torr Vale Mill) and the railway. Lowes Mill and the railway station were badly damaged and shop windows in New Mills' Market Street and Union Street were smashed. The other plane dropped two bombs on Woodside Street close to the railway viaduct. The bombers then began dropping incendiaries and machine gunned the cricket ground in Church Road, although local lads playing in a cricket match there between Hayfield and Birch Vale were unhurt. Two bombs were then dropped on Low Leighton Road in the neighbouring village of Low Leighton, destroying the Methodist Chapel and killing one person in adjacent houses (Whitefield Villas) which were wrecked. The Ollersett View hospital building opposite the chapel was also blasted and left with shattered windows and holes in the roof. Following the Sett Valley to Hayfield they bombed three cottages in Valley Road which were demolished, and six people were killed. Ten others were injured and there were over 150 incidents of damage to property. Rowarth escaped with a few broken windows, some smashed bottles of spirits in the Little Mill pub, plus several slates from the roof and some shattered windows at Laneside Farm. The German planes then headed out east over Kinder and dropped their last bombs over Darlton Quarry in Stoney Middleton, damaging a blacksmith's shop and a crusher shed, before strafing Chatsworth House and finally escaping. They flew so low over the quarry that leaves were blown off the trees. By now, however, RAF 12 Group Fighter Command Control in Lincolnshire was fully aware of their presence and four Spitfires from the renowned Polish 303 squadron at RAF Kirton in Lindsey were scrambled to deal with the intruders. There was still a good deal of low cloud and as one Spitfire opened fire to deflect the Germans' attention the others attacked from above. Both Ju 88s were taken by surprise and had no time to take cover in the higher cloud above them. One of the German planes, with both its engines on fire, crashed in flames on a farm killing all four crew. The second plane crash-landed at another farm nearby. All four crew escaped and ran away but were quickly captured by the local Home Guard.

Farming was having its usual tough time and the Ministry of Agriculture felt that the harvest of 1942 could well be critical for the country. Farmers were also being asked to give detailed crop plans for 1943. Once again there was a threatened shortage of agricultural labourers as male workers were conscripted but the Women's Land Army was working hard to make up the shortfall. It had proved itself in the Great War so there was much less prejudice and resistance from farmers. In the more remote parts of Derbyshire farmers' wives and daughters had been doing farm work for years anyway. There was concern, however, that some farms were being compelled to grow crops for which their farms were either ecologically or economically unsuited. Dairy farming and crop growing were suitable for the more southerly fertile parts of Derbyshire but in the Dark Peak the soil tended to be thin and of poor quality, mostly fit only for grazing sheep. Sheep and poultry farming had declined generally but not much in Derbyshire where there were fewer farming options. During the Great War fresh eggs had been more freely available and in the Eastern Counties there had been concerted efforts to expand and promote the poultry industry. Although meeting with some success, keeping hens continued to remain what it had always been, more of a cottage industry. The inevitable result was that when war came there was an acute shortage of eggs once again; in the Great War four fresh eggs per week per adult had been the allowance, now it was only one fresh egg per week. The absence of fresh eggs was partly compensated by dried eggs and one of the most frequent complaints about food during the Second World War concerned dried eggs. Dried-egg powder was imported from America and one tin was the equivalent of a dozen fresh egg. The powder was used in cake mixes or recipes where the taste was disguised but its use for scrambled eggs, omelettes, or in egg-based sandwich spreads, was often disliked and the one fresh egg a week which was allowed was much treasured by people. Government attempts to extoll the virtues of dried egg fell on deaf ears and many people simply preferred to go without them.

A month after the outbreak of the war, the Ministry of Agriculture had coined the slogan 'Dig for Victory', the inspiration for which they had borrowed from the Great War when David Lloyd George had urged the population towards self-sufficiency. This was followed up by a poster advertising campaign, jingoism in the forms of song and poetry, and a number of advice booklets on what to grow, when to grow it, and how to grow fruit and vegetables efficiently. One Ministry booklet carried a picture of a toddler on the front dragging a small spade and hoe with him and carried the message that no one was too young to help. Vegetables were divided into three rough categories. Group A: root crops, included potatoes, carrots and parsnips; Group B: winter greens, included cabbage, kale and sprouts, and Group C: termed miscellaneous, included peas, beans, onions and tomatoes. Gooseberries, red and black currants were harvested from bushes in cottage gardens. Blackberries and raspberries grew wild and were often picked by children. In Clowne the children would also go fruit picking or potato picking on the farms in the school holidays for which they would receive a small wage for each basket picked (3*d*; now worth about 65p). The general aim was to ensure a year-round supply of fresh fruit and vegetables so certain fresh foods were actively promoted. A homemade drink called Carrolade, made from the juices of carrots and swedes, was advocated as well as curried carrots and carrot jam. Potato skins were deemed most nutritious and folk were encouraged to eat them, whether baked or boiled. Lord Woolton, Minister of Food 1940–1943, had the job of promoting the benefits of rationing to the public. One result of this had been his favourite 'Woolton Pie' of diced carrots, potatoes, swedes, and cauliflower, spring onions, vegetable extract and oatmeal. Spam, a word whose meaning has changed entirely in the twenty-first century, was a compressed bacon-based luncheon meat imported from America and sold in small loaf-shaped tins. It could be eaten hot or cold. Maconochies, who had made tinned meat and vegetable stew for the troops, also manufactured Spam at their Glossop base. Nevertheless, there were shortages of certain fresh foods, especially lemons, bananas and oranges. Oranges were in short supply and usually reserved for pregnant women and children. Lemons and bananas were unobtainable, and this resulted in a revival of the old Great War song 'Yes! We have no bananas.' Even apples, which were homegrown, were often a rarity. A Buxton lad, sent by his mother to do the day's shopping, spent most of the shopping money on fresh apples which had recently arrived. When he arrived home he expected his parents to be angry with him, but this was not the case because fresh fruit of any type was a comparatively rare luxury, at least in the towns. Much of the fruit which was available, including apples, pears, plums, gooseberries and blackcurrants, was expected to be used for preserving which housewives were expected to do themselves. Extra rations of precious sugar carefully done up in blue bags, were allocated to those making jams and jellies and chutneys according to the amount produced. Quince jam and mint jelly were among favourites although these are no longer very popular. Apple and tomato chutneys were also favourites, and have remained so, although today most chutneys are factory made.

However, food rationing continued to cause grief. Folk in rural Derbyshire seldom ate out, so there were complaints that in the towns and cities (such as Chesterfield, Matlock, Bakewell, Ashbourne and Derby) those who could afford to eat in restaurants could supplement their rations at the expense of those who couldn't. Consequently, in May the Ministry of Food ordered new restrictions. Restaurant meals were to consist of no more than three courses and only one dish in one of these courses could contain fish, meat or poultry. A maximum price of 5s (about £10) was set for meals, and no meals were to be served in public catering establishments between 11 pm and 5 am without a special licence. Churchill had already ordered the setting up of British Restaurants shortly after the war had begun, on the model of Lloyd George's Community Kitchens in the Great War, where a decent three-course meal could be obtained for 9d (£1.50). Although rural Derbyshire had missed out (due to lack of numbers and transport), some Derbyshire towns had benefitted.

In December 1939 scientists at Cambridge University had carried out an experiment with rations. For three months they, and a group of volunteers, limited themselves to 1 egg, 1lb (0.495kg) of meat and 4oz of fat (0.125kg) per week, ¼ pint of milk (0.14 litre) per day, with unlimited potatoes, vegetables and wholemeal bread. During this time, they carried out similar strenuous physical work to that done by ordinary members of the population. After three months they found that their health and productivity remained excellent. A similar experiment was carried out three years ago with two healthy adults living for a week in winter on rations from the Great War and the result was the same. Both adults were amazed at how healthy they felt afterwards. The lessons learned were that, in both wars, rationing improved the health of British people; the diseases of malnutrition were eradicated; infant mortality declined; and life expectancy rose; for the simple reason that everyone had a varied diet with plenty of vitamins and mineral traces, and that large quantities of food were not necessary to provide an adequate healthy diet.

As in the Great War the potential female work force was of great strategic importance. The numbers of men conscripted into the Forces once again opened up unlimited job opportunities for women to again fill the roles that had been reoccupied by men during the interwar years. Women now worked in the production areas of factories as well as on the less skilled and monotonous assembly lines. Female workers were popular in industry because they could be paid far less than men and so labour costs could be reduced. The Women's Land Army had been resurrected with great success. It was a healthy outdoor life which broke down class barriers, albeit the hours were long and often cold or wet, and the work hard and dirty. On the canals, which became so vital for transport, communications and supplies after petrol rationing and the armed forces' requisitioning of trains and motor transport, female workers transported coal and munitions supplies across Britain on the narrow boats; an arduous task, especially working the large numbers of locks. They were called the Idle Women by numbers of men in a play on the initials 'IW' which stood for Inland Waterways. After female conscription in 1941 numbers of women left their previous civilian jobs. The Midland Drapery in Derby lost four-fifths of its female workforce practically overnight. Munitions was a major industry for female workers and 3,000 women took jobs in the Derby munitions industry. The LMS employed women as carters and the LNER employed women to manufacture concrete railway sleepers while Derby got its first woman police constable. Women also took on paid military jobs and responsibilities in the ATS, the WRNS and the WAAF where before voluntary service had been relied upon to do the work. Initially these were support roles such as those of cook, clerk, cleaner or communications; but gradually extended to include those of mechanic, armourer, searchlight and anti-aircraft instrument operators. Subsequently, women were allowed to work at the top secret decoding establishment of Bletchley and to join the Special Operations Executive (SOE) and work as secret agents and radio operators in Nazi occupied Europe. However, despite this high level of involvement in the war effort workforce, very few women belonged to a union and most of the male workforce didn't want them as members in case pay differentials were jeopardised. The old Victorian prejudices remained alive and well.

Childcare, and its expense, had long been a perennial problem for working mothers, and the wartime coalition government did realise this to a large extent, especially with the support of Ernest Bevin. Cheaper school meals were introduced in the hope of preventing children returning home for lunch as well as ensuring they got a good square midday meal. Bevin was more of a realist than some more traditionalist members and he understood that if the government insisted upon conscripting mothers to work, the problem of childcare could not just be dismissed as 'their problem'. Consequently, by 1943, some 1,345 government sponsored childcare nurseries had been established compared with just 14 available in 1940. In mainly rural Derbyshire, however, because of the many isolated locations and the lack of transport, especially in the Peak District, it meant that more often than not female contribution was in the role of housewife, homemaker, mother and carer. In the villages or on the farms any childcare required was usually provided by female friends and relatives. Nevertheless the importance of these home-based roles was recognised, especially as those who stayed at home grew vegetables, knitted comforts for the troops, and performed essential public and social services for the Women's Voluntary Service (WVS). The WVS would basically do anything which was required of them from dispensing tea and sympathy, finding billets for evacuated children, running rest centres, to organising meals, helping those in need and giving first aid. In Crich parish, for example, there were WVS first aid exercises where children would be given labels with their supposed injuries and told to report to the WVS centre for 'treatment', while adult WVS members would mock up injuries on themselves with dirt and lipstick and then present themselves as 'casualties'. The WVS proved themselves to be very efficient, effective and caring, and they were often referred to as 'the army that Hitler forgot.' The role of housewife had become a 'patriotic duty' and even the government acknowledged that 'the house-wife has become a heroine in the defeat of Hitler'. There were, of course, all the usual mutterings and women's pay was still far less than that given to a man for the same job, but women were determined to play their part in the war as well, if not better, than they had done in the Great War.

The trades unions' action and calls for better pay and conditions had improved matters for female workers but only in proportion. Many female workers still earned around a third less than male workers for the same job. In the House of Commons Dr Edith Summerskill led a call for equal pay for women. She stated that in the auxiliary services women were replacing men 'head for head' but, although men were asking and obtaining the going rate for the jobs, women were paid well below that rate at only two-thirds of the rate which the men received. Yet members of the ATS worked as dispatchers, electricians, motor mechanics and cyclists; those in the WRNS did clerical work, dispatch riding, wireless work and motor transport; and women in the WAAF worked as wireless mechanics, electricians, aircraft hands and armament assistants. In addition, it was suggested that there should be a special wartime domestic corps for women with its own uniform. Dr Summerskill also said arguments put to her that women would deprive men of jobs in a competitive labour market were rubbish. Surely, she said,

ATS members, Derbyshire, c1941.

it was efficiency not sex which should be the benchmark. The calling up of women in the 45–50 age group was criticised as well when it was felt that there were younger women who could be called upon, but the government had in mind nursing, midwifery and hospital services which required older women with more experience. This raised further protests that jobs seen as 'women's work' were traditionally low paid which was why there was now a shortage of midwives, nurses, and servants.

The government remained keenly aware of the fact that British society was far from equal. There had been no 'land fit for heroes' after the Great War, only another two decades of austerity, and this was causing severe problems for millions of people who had already given all of what little they had. There was also a strong perception that the more wealthy sections of society were not paying their fair share. In an attempt to address the problems, and to keep low income workers and the poorer sections of society on side, Sir William Beveridge had been commissioned to write a report proposing the beginnings of a social security system. This report was published on 1 December and its basis was to 'introduce a system of social insurance from cradle to grave.' Beveridge believed that all workers should pay a weekly contribution which would then be paid back in benefits to cover sickness, unemployment, retirement or being widowed. The main points of his report were:

- 'Proposals for the future should not be limited by "sectional interests" in learning from experience and that a "revolutionary moment in the world's history is a time for revolutions, not for patching."'
- Social insurance is only one part of a 'comprehensive policy of social progress'. The five giants on the road to reconstruction were Want, Disease, Ignorance, Squalor and Idleness.
- Policies of social security 'must be achieved by co-operation between the State and the individual', with the state securing the service and contributions. The state 'should not stifle incentive, opportunity, responsibility; in establishing a national minimum, it should leave room and encouragement for voluntary action by each individual to provide more than that minimum for himself and his family'.

There was already free hospital treatment available for war casualties, but this was laying the groundwork for the introduction of a National Health Service and Beveridge argued, against much opposition, that the recommendations in his report would also provide a minimum standard of living. To guarantee this a minimum wage was needed, which was the ultimate dream of workers, trades unionists and strikers. However, many in the middle and upper classes still felt this might encourage fecklessness and recklessness among the working classes.

There was, however, tremendous admiration, sympathy and fellow feeling for the Red Army as they fought hard against fascism and inflicted heavy losses on the Germans. An 'Aid to Russia' Fund was started by the Derby TGWU with a donation of £5 (£210) and Derby held a 'Russia Week' in June which raised £1,150 (£48,220). Derby Labour Party and Derby Trades Council went on to raise twice that amount between 1942–1944. Food, fuel, clothes, munitions and equipment were sent from all over the county to help Russia in her struggles. Anti-communist feelings were forgotten, at least temporarily. Communist Party membership increased. There were 150 Communist Party members in Derby alone, a third of whom worked at Rolls Royce. However, when affiliation to the Labour Party was suggested it proved to be a step too far and the TGWU led the opposition to it. After the war was over, and Stalin's purges came to light, the Communist Party lost a great deal of support and sympathy in Britain. The Germans hated the Russians and behaved with callous cruelty towards them. Russian women were beaten and raped. Russian men, especially soldiers, were executed or sent to concentration camps where many of them died. A Russian soldier who tried to escape from the German concentration camp on Alderney in the Channel Islands was crucified on the camp gates.

From the other side of the globe, by Christmastime this year, there were 60,000 American GIs in Britain, regarded in many quarters as 'over-sexed, over-paid and over here', who had arrived late and missed much of the action. In turn many of the Americans regarded Britain as a quaint, shabby rather backward country with obsessions of class differentiation and tea drinking. The authorities, attempting to make relations more cordial, suggested that as the GIs were far from home it would be nice if British families would invite them to spend Christmas Day in their homes. They would not be expected to feed them from their own meagre rations as each GI would be issued with a provision pack for his hosts. These included spam, coffee, biscuits, cake, chocolate, tinned peaches and soups. They also brought presents of nylons, chocolates, whisky and cigarettes, commodities mostly no longer available in Britain, with chewing gum and comics for the children. Initially the British were overwhelmed but a little wary. The film *Yanks*, made in the 1970s on the Derbyshire borders, has a scene in which a young GI spends Christmas Day with his English girlfriend's family. His girlfriend's mother unwraps his gift to her of a Christmas cake painfully slowly, undoing the string and winding it into a ball, then carefully folding the wrapping paper, before she finally lifts the lid of the box to reveal the cake. She is astonished at seeing such a rich cake and what she believes is so much ostentation. She acknowledges her thanks to him very briefly before carefully replacing the cake in its box, and with the lid firmly back in place, puts it aside. It is probably an uncomfortably accurate depiction of many first such meetings, but it was not all bad. The GIs told their hosts about Christmas at home and of the Christmas customs of advent calendars and hanging ginger biscuits on the Christmas tree. Their British hosts swapped tales and explained about Christmas crackers which most GIs had not seen before. Most of the American bases were in East Anglia, and so having a GI to Christmas dinner in Derbyshire was uncommon, although there were a few instances in the Derby area and some Derbyshire families had relatives in East Anglia who regularly entertained young GIs at Christmastime in the latter part of the war.

CHAPTER FIVE

1943

The focus on the war and the effort needed to support it had tended to block out the fact that some things carried on as normal despite the war, ordinary civilian life didn't just come to a stop. After the Great War it had been recognised that more water for drinking, washing, domestic and industrial use was urgently needed by the cities of Derby, Leicester, Sheffield and Manchester and, since this had become a matter approaching urgency in the early 1930s, action was needed. In 1935 the decision was taken to expand the Howden and Derwent reservoir chain (built 1900–1916) in the Upper Derwent Valley by building a third reservoir in the valley that would flood the Derbyshire villages of Derwent (named after the shallow river which flowed through the village) and neighbouring Ashopton (named after the River Ashop) which lay very close to the border with Yorkshire. Work had begun in 1935 with the building of the Ashopton and Ladybower viaducts which would carry the two main roads over the proposed reservoir. The outbreak of war had a knock-on effect in making the supplies of raw materials scarcer and more expensive, and also depriving the labour force of its younger and fitter workers as they enlisted in the Armed Forces. The need to maintain and increase water supply did not diminish, however, and work continued albeit at a slower pace.

Sheffield, the nearest of the cities to the scheme, was becoming increasingly targeted by the Luftwaffe because of its industries, notably the steel industry, and evacuation of Sheffield schools was becoming a pressing necessity. In the summer of 1940, one Sheffield girls' convent school had decided that Derwent Hall would be a suitable place to which they could evacuate, large enough to board all the girls, and close enough to Sheffield for the pupils not to lose touch with their families. The Hall, built in 1672, was large, rambling, damp and draughty, but it was comparatively safe. It also had its own chapel, for Sunday worship, and large gardens which would be suitable for games and physical education activities. Beds, desks, blackboards, kitchenware, equipment, everything that the school might need, had to be brought in; but by September 1940, it was ready for 140 girls and 8 teachers to move in. Conditions were rather spartan being cramped, often

SFD 8   DERWENT DAM. DERBYSHIRE   Photo by J. F. LAWRENCE

Derwent Reservoir in full flow, c1943.

cold, and there was no hot water, but this bothered the adults rather more than it bothered many of the children. Meanwhile work on the dams had continued and the girls could see the effects from the Hall. One wrote how the Hall 'dominated the small stone-built village...in the centre of which was a picturesque pack-horse bridge...' However, in August of 1941, the school had returned to Sheffield. The stress of the living conditions had taken its toll on the staff and some of the pupils, and the intention remained to flood Derwent and its smaller neighbour, Ashopton, as soon as possible. The flooding was to go ahead despite numerous voluble protests, not least from those who had won new-found rights to hike freely in the hills after the Kinder trespass of 1932. The Ashopton Inn which had stood on the old road between Sheffield and Manchester (the new viaduct carrying the A57 over the valley rising immediately behind it) was a popular inn with locals, walkers, and transport services, and its impending loss was loudly lamented. Derwent was a working village and there were several farms in the area. Despite this, the final service in Derwent church was held on 17 March 1943, just four days before the formation of 617 Squadron (of 'Dambusters' fame) under the command of Guy Gibson. Afterwards the destruction of the village began in earnest: buildings were demolished; the packhorse bridge was dismantled, but rebuilt close to the Howden Reservoir; bodies from the churchyard were disinterred and reburied in nearby Bamford churchyard. Flooding of the valley began in the autumn of 1943, but it took two years and by the time it was completed the war was over. The Luftwaffe must have been aware of the dams in the

VALENTINE'S "AIRCRAFT RECOGNITION" CARDS

VALENTINE & SONS, LTD.,
DUNDEE and LONDON.
Printed in Gt. Britain.

Avro Manchester, Second World War.

Derwent Valley but had failed to recognise their significance. Flying at night over the Pennines was not an easy business in the days when altimeters could be disastrously unreliable at times, so the reservoirs might not have been a notable priority for German aircrew trying to navigate their way over uncertain terrain, often in poor weather conditions, to reach their targets of population centres and industrial complexes.

In the spring of 1943 Derbyshire played a critical part in the preparations for Operation Chastise, better known as the Dambusters, the collective name of those who took part in it. A decision had been taken to attack the industrialised Ruhr Valley in Germany which provided hydroelectric power for German industry and homes as well as water for German canals, for German steel-making and for drinking. The idea was to breach the Möhne, Edersee and Sorpe dams causing catastrophic damage and flooding, hitting at the heart of the German war industry. The attack had to be low level, accurate and a 'one-off surprise' for the dams were well defended and had torpedo nets to protect them. Barnes Wallis, who worked for Vickers, worked on developing a 'bouncing bomb'. By bouncing across the water until it reached its target it could avoid both underwater and surface defences. When the bomb reached its target, it would sink and explode rather like a depth charge. Avro Lancaster bombers were chosen for the job and a new squadron, 617, was formed, led by Wing Commander Guy Gibson. However, Gibson and his colleagues needed to practise low level flying in similar conditions to those they would face targeting the dams in the Ruhr Valley. The Derwent

Howden Reservoir with Margery Hill centre background.

Valley in Derbyshire had a chain of three reservoirs: Ladybower (not flooded until autumn 1943), the Derwent, and the Howden, with four dams and two viaducts. Although Ladybower wasn't fully flooded until 1945, the Derwent and Howden reservoirs provided ideal training territory for 617 Squadron. Each dam has twin towers (one on either side) and the Howden dam, the oldest of the three dams and the furthest up the valley, faces the barren moorlands of Bleaklow and Margery Hill, both of which claimed crashed planes and loss of life in the Second World War. For a couple of months 617 Squadron practised low-flying the Lancasters up and down the Derwent Valley reservoirs until they were satisfied that they could accomplish their mission. Operation Chastise caused catastrophic flooding of the Ruhr and Eder valleys; killing 1,600 civilians, destroying two hydroelectric power stations, and causing severe damage to factories, mines and other power stations. Although it is now seventy-five years (in 2018) since the Dambusters mission, its anniversary is still celebrated by a Lancaster plane flying between the twin towers, low over the dams, recreating an iconic image of the Second World War.

Meanwhile, the curse of the Dark Peak aircraft wrecks had returned to Derbyshire with a vengeance. On 26 January, Wellington Mk.III X3348/ZL-Z, was returning from an attack on the port of Lorient in France when it crashed on Kinder Scout, fortunately on a piece of level moorland which meant that the crew of six were almost unhurt. The plane was not so fortunate and became a 'write-off'. Four days later two crashes occurred in one day. An ill-fated training exercise from Wymeswold, near Loughborough, took place in bad weather involving low cloud and snow showers. Wellington MK.IC R1011/M crashed on Birchen Bank Moss up on Bleaklow. It was a bad time of year. Three of the crew died and the remaining two needed treatment for exposure as well as their injuries. Another plane from the same training exercise, Wellington Mk.III X3941, also came down in the bad weather, hitting a row of trees close to Darley Dale near Matlock and crashing in a nearby field, killing two of the crew and injuring three others. This was followed in mid-February by two crashes near Hope. The first, Wellington Mk.III HF613/DD-R, became caught up in a blizzard on a cross-country flight, and crashed into a river near the village before striking a steep embankment and killing all five crew. The second one, Airspeed Oxford MK.I DF485, was on a training exercise from Ashbourne. Becoming disorientated and having problems with severe turbulence, the pilot crash-landed in a field between Hope and Castleton. No one was hurt and the plane was not badly damaged. Night training exercises continued to take their toll and Airspeed Oxford Mk.I BG197 crashed in woods near Matlock on the night of 3 March, killing its pilot after he became disorientated and descended too early. Five weeks later, on another night-training exercise from Ashbourne, Blenheim Mk.IV V6078, struck trees and crashed into a field near Matlock, killing all three crew. In March Miles Master Mk.III W8761 crash-landed at Great Hucklow near Tideswell when it hit bad weather during a formation flying practice; the crew were unhurt. Wellington Mk.III DF611/W was on an infra-red bombing exercise when the engines developed a fault. The pilot attempted a landing in open country but the aircraft overran the Buxton-Ashbourne road and hit a wall where it burst into flames leaving three of the crew dead and two injured. Edale claimed another victim towards the end of April when a USAAF plane, P-47C Thunderbolt 41-6277, crashed after suffering turbulence in a thunderstorm and nose-diving into the ground near Upper Booth. Although the pilot bailed out he was injured by a bad landing. Oxford Mk.I EB717/XT was yet another night-flight victim. It should have been a routine flight but the pilot became disorientated and shortly after sunrise the aircraft, now off course, flew into low cloud near Buxton and struck a stone wall on Burbage Edge which killed the pilot and badly damaged the aircraft. The day afterwards, 13 May, Armstrong Whitworth Whitley MK.V EB338 was on a short cross-country training flight when one of the engines failed. The instructor managed to crash-land the plane but it hit a wall alongside the Buxton-Ashbourne railway and tore up some railway track before coming to rest in a field. One crew member was killed and five seriously injured. Wellington Mk.IC DV678 had to make a forced landing at Chatsworth Park near Bakewell after suffering engine failure but all six crew only suffered slight injuries. In October Handley Page Halifax Mk.II HR727/MH-V had taken part in a bombing raid on Frankfurt and was returning to base. One of the engines and one of the fuel tanks had been damaged by enemy fire and the radio subsequently failed as a result of the batteries running down and the aircraft generator being unable to recharge them. By now the weather had closed in with low cloud and rain making visibility impaired. Fuel was running low and the pilot cautiously began to descend in the hope of seeing landmarks only to fly straight into the ground on Blackden Edge near Edale. Five of the seven crew died. Later that same month Airspeed Oxford MK.I LX518 on a night-training flight claimed another victim. The pilot was on a solo flight. However, bad weather rapidly closed in, as so often in the Pennines, and he became lost and disorientated, eventually crashing into Margery Hill on the far side of the Howden Reservoir in the Derwent Valley. He did not survive the experience. A fortnight before Christmas a USAAF plane, P-38J Lightning 42-67480, on its way from Preston to Northamptonshire, found itself in trouble when one engine failed and the other engine overheated. The pilot attempted a crash-landing in a field at Cronkstone Grange near Buxton but the plane hit a wall and caught fire. Amazingly the pilot was able to walk away uninjured. There were other air mishaps as well, of which scant detail is known, in what proved to be a bumper year for aircraft being wrecked in the High Peak.

There had been recent serious strikes in the transport industry and also by the dockers of Liverpool and Birkenhead. These had not actually involved Derbyshire but there was obviously a 'knock-on' effect and the Minister of Labour, Ernest Bevin, as leader of the TGWU, suffered acute embarrassment. In addition, by the middle of 1943 the mining industry was short staffed and in desperate need of 40,000 miners, which directly affected much of southern Derbyshire. Coal production had slumped and by December Britain had just three weeks' supply of coal in reserve. Voluntary requests for new miners had made little impact so Ernest Bevin introduced a scheme whereby a proportion

Looking across the Howden Reservoir to Margery Hill and the remote Derbyshire moors beyond which claimed several plane crash victims in the Second World War.

of conscripted men would work in the mines instead of being drafted into the armed forces. This was done by means of a ballot. As a result, 48,000 'Bevin boys' were sent to work down the mines. Half had been selected by ballot, which denied any choice of serving in the armed forces, and half were volunteers who preferred mining to the armed forces. The ballot was simple. Every month a number was drawn from a hat and all men whose National Service Registration Number ended with the same number were sent down the mines. Refusal to accept could mean a fine or imprisonment. The 'Bevin boys' were sent to work in the various coal mines of England, Wales and Scotland, and represented about 10 per cent of those aged 18–25 called up during the last two years of the war. There was a great deal of resentment among those chosen, especially for those young lads who had dreamed of honour in the armed services it was a bitter disappointment. There was also the added frustration of misunderstanding by the public. Mining was a vital necessity to the war, but many saw it as an opt-out from combatant service; although it could be equally dangerous to fighting at the Fronts. There were a number of coal mines in Derbyshire, especially around the Chesterfield area, notably Alfreton and Swanwick in the Amber Valley, and in the Bolsover district, including Bolsover, Cresswell, Glapwell, South Normanton and Shirebrook. Mining conscripts came from all classes and all regions. Newly recruited miners received their initial training at a number of government training centres, mostly in England, where they received a basic six weeks of training before being sent down the mines. Conscripts usually lived in Nissen huts adjacent to the mines where they worked. The initial experience of descending hundreds of feet below ground to work in the cramped, silent, airless, twilight of middle-earth must have been terrifying, especially for those who suffered from claustrophobia. Most worked with the pit ponies or on the conveyor belts alongside more experienced men, but some worked at the coalface. In the Second World War there were few mechanical aids and it is an understatement to say that the work was hard, dangerous, dirty and unrelenting, for both men and animals.

There were now fresh problems in industry involving unions and management. As a way of involving workers in more participation Joint Production Committees (JPCs) had first been set up in 1942, and by 1943, there were 4,000 of them. The aim was 'maximisation of output and minimisation of conflict'. One of the problems during the earlier part of the war was that employees could work up to 100 hours a week, which was too much. Attempts were made to reduce the working week to sixty hours and to ensure those working over that number of hours were exempt from fire-watching duties. Although many improvements in wages and conditions were achieved, the JPCs became a vehicle for more union militancy. This was not entirely of their own making but more borne out of the desire for business interests to make ever larger profits. Efficiency and effectiveness were key words in providing for the needs of the war. The government had a 'cost plus' system for contracts with private industry, which worked on 'a basis of the cost of the work plus a percentage for profits. Therefore, the higher the cost, the higher the profits.' So it paid to use workers on overtime or at weekends when their rates were higher than during normal working hours. This gave the JPCs a golden opportunity in terms of involvement and an excellent bargaining position, the significance of which was not lost on them. The Derbyshire mining industry in particular benefitted and there were less problems with Derbyshire miners than elsewhere in the country. They gained wage rises and war bonuses and some improvement in working conditions. Grassmoor Colliery, close to Chesterfield, was the first colliery to provide pit-head baths for miners and a workers' canteen. However, Monday morning absenteeism was still proving a problem, but Derbyshire miners did not care to be reminded of this, and the unions were careful to avoid conflict with their members, so it was left to the pit owners themselves to take appropriate action against those who were late or missed their shifts altogether. However, it was not all bad news. Denby, near Belper, although rather better known for its pottery industry and being the birthplace of John Flamsteed, the first Astronomer Royal, boasted an absenteeism rate of only 6 per cent for its colliery workers. However, the declining productivity of Derbyshire mines during the first years of the war was more due to the lack of numbers as a result of conscription, or young miners leaving for surface jobs with similar rates of pay, rather than the miners working inefficiently. The fall in numbers had been responsible for the Bevin Boys scheme to recruit more miners, albeit not necessarily willing miners.

For the 1943 Wakes (a week or fortnight when all the factories and offices closed in the towns to enable employees to take their annual holiday) Glossopians decided on what is now known as a 'staycation'. They opted to stay at home to save on transport, fuel and hard-earned cash, and also to try and avoid the bombing attacks. Impressed, Glossop Town Council decided to organise a 'fortnight of fun at home'. The highlight was a cricket match at the North Road ground with two teams of county cricketers which included stars from Lancashire, Derbyshire, Somerset, Sussex, Gloucester, and Leicester. In Manor Park there were concerts by Glossop Old Band, the Manhattan Follies and a display by the men of the Home Guard; and on Norfolk Square a concert was given by the band of Third Battalion of the Sherwood Foresters'. Whist drives, other concerts, dances and beetle drives were also held. Many of the Derbyshire villages, hamlets, and remote farmsteads followed Glossop's example in staying at home as well, but they were not generally subject to the Wakes system and farm animals still needed to be fed and milked daily. Local scout groups across the county from Glossop to Youlgreave to Derby were active in local community activities and they helped out with harvesting, collecting paper for the war effort, or any other jobs that needed doing.

Children all over the Derbyshire countryside helped out with the harvest, which was great fun for them. Although the work was hard and tiring, it took their minds off the war for a while.

The 1st Derbyshire Yeomanry had been in Tunisia since late 1942 and were joined in January 1943 by the 2nd Battalion and the 2/5th Battalion, now renamed the 5th Battalion, of the Sherwood Foresters. There was fierce fighting for control of the Tunisian coast and reaching Tunis was finally accomplished in March. Subsequently both the 5th Battalion and the 1st Derbyshire Yeomanry were sent to Italy; where the 5th Battalion took part in the assault landing at Salerno in September 1943. Both units fought around Monte Cassino where the 5th Battalion sustained heavy casualties.

Christmas in Derbyshire in 1943 was a very 'make do and mend' affair. Virtually all presents were homemade and there was still an acute shortage of paper. There were no chickens or geese; a bit of mutton if folk were lucky and, of course in rural Derbyshire, rabbits and birds still made it into the pot. However, most Christmas food was 'mock' or 'fake', made to look like the real thing when it was far from the real thing. Any kind of meat with potatoes and parsnips was regarded as a treat. Christmas puddings were virtually non-existent so jam roly-poly or spotted dick were often substituted, with a white sauce or custard poured over. Although milk was rationed no-one was going to notice if the odd pint here and there made its way to someone's Christmas table; or, if they did, no one was going to complain. Out in the Derbyshire countryside it was doubtful that anyone would even know. Folk tuned in to the radio for the Christmas broadcast by the king but otherwise entertainment was made by the people themselves. After lunch there might be a family walk, if the weather was suitable, or listening to a concert given by a local band. Children played ball games or tag (a game where one person is 'it' and has to tag or touch someone else as the other children run around in all directions or hide to avoid being tagged. If anyone is touched they become the new 'it'). In the evenings board games, like snakes and ladders or Ludo, and non-gambling card games would be played; stories would be read or told by firelight or lamplight. Many more isolated homes did not have electricity and lighting would be by a paraffin lamp, Tilley lamp, or candles. Carols would be sung, and if anyone had a piano there might be a 'jolly knees up' with folk singing and dancing as someone played traditional tunes. In the more remote corners of Derbyshire celebrating Christmas in this manner did not end with the war and continued into the 1950s and 1960s.

CHAPTER SIX

1944

By the beginning of 1944 many were 'war weary' and wondering again just when it would all end. It was not a good year for industry and the TUC came under criticism because 1944 marked a massive number of wartime strike actions. There were over 2,000 strikes which involved the loss of nearly 4 million days working production. It was a staggering number and it could obviously not continue if Britain were to win the war. Churchill reacted angrily by imposing Defence Regulation 1AA making incitement to strike illegal. In this he was actually supported by the TUC who felt that some of their members had gone too far and were holding the country to ransom and saw the threat of crippling essential production by withholding their labour as a form of blackmail. Early in the war there had been many genuine grievances, but the TUC felt that the concessions granted had gone to the heads of a few and that all negotiations for wages and better conditions should now wait until the war was over. There were plenty of signs that the tide was finally turning and that 'all hands on deck' should be the order of the day. Nationally the unions had doubled their membership during the war and by 1944 almost half the workforce was engaged in some type of war work. Industrial militancy began to rear its head once more but this time many of the protagonists were women and apprentices. The effect was dramatic. In 1940 the number of days lost through strike action was 940,000. By 1944 this had risen to a staggering 3,710,000, only outdone by the number of strike days lost in 1917. There were still many grievances to be settled. Derby, Long Eaton, Ilkeston and Ripley all had branches of the Operative Bakers' Union. This local dispute involved the District Secretary, who had terminated an agreement with the Co-operative Society against his colleagues' wishes, which resulted in a vote of no confidence, so he demanded Union reimbursement. 'Storm in a teacup' seemed to sum up the situation. However, there were far more serious issues at stake and several organisations won considerable pay rises for both male and female workers; among them the hosiery and narrow fabrics industries and the Amalgamated Society of Textile workers involving staff in Wirksworth,

Matlock and Bakewell. The National Union of Teachers (NUT) in Derbyshire was concerned at the low levels of staffing in Derbyshire, insisting it would not improve until salaries were raised. Higher wages tend to have a knock-on effect in that if one section of workers wins a substantial pay rise then other sections of workers expect to follow suit.

The education minister, R.A. Butler, was charged with steering the Education Act 1944 through Parliament. There had long been concern over access to education for children from the working classes and poorer sections of society, particularly in the northern cities, and folk were more aware than ever that a decent education system for every child would be essential for future generations to cope with an increasingly complex and mechanised world. It was also recognised that girls would have to be included in this plan as well. Females had demonstrated in both World Wars that they were just as capable as men of working at different jobs and contributing to society and that they could no longer be relegated to the kitchen hearth or the nursery. This new innovative legislation would provide more time at school and free secondary education for all children without all the hidden costs and inequalities that would affect poorer children. Under the Act, Local Education Authorities (LEAs) were required to submit proposals for the reorganisation of secondary education into three main categories: grammar, secondary and technical as recommended by Sir William Spens' report in 1938. Allocation to a particular category would be by means of an examination taken at 11 years old which would be subsequently known as the 11+ exam. The intention was to provide equal opportunities for all children through a tri-partite

Old Silk Mill, Derby, c1940s.

system of education. There would always be differentials in the potential of children. Some would be more academically inclined while others would be more practically minded. Most parents who could not afford to let all their children stay at school usually favoured boys over girls because there were far more opportunities available for boys and because of the frequently mistaken notion that most girls' ambitions were simply to marry and have children. The school leaving age was also raised to 15 with a recommendation that it should be raised to 16 after the war.

Juvenile delinquency had remained a problem, although not so much in rural areas like parts of Derbyshire, and the government now required all young people over 16 to register and offered them an increasing number of options including clubs and organisations which they could join and take part in activities. Again, in the more rural parts of Derbyshire, transport to these resources was going to be a problem, especially with petrol rationing in force. The usual reasons given for delinquency included absent fathers, working mothers, lax discipline and watching the wrong kind of films; but young people have rebelled against their elders since time immemorial. However, in wartime vandalism was just an expensive and unwanted nuisance. It was essential that the enemy was not inadvertently given a helping hand by youths being stupid. Besides, the importance of the young replacement generation had long been recognised and there was great incentive to ensure that they were well-trained and educated to cope with the demands of an increasingly difficult world.

Long Eaton before the Second World War.

Dame Laura Knight, a celebrated female war artist of the Second World War, was born Laura Johnson at Long Eaton in the south of Derbyshire. Her painting was in the English Impressionism style and realist tradition. She was made a Dame in 1929, and in 1936 'she became the first woman elected to full membership of the Royal Academy.' She was already 62 when the Second World War broke out and she had previously done a couple of war paintings on themes of sport and physical training in the Great War. At the outbreak of the Second World War she was commissioned to paint a recruitment poster for the Women's Land Army and this was followed by other commissions from the WAAF and the WAAC, mostly of female military personnel and civilian war workers. In total she produced seventeen paintings for the WAAC and after the war, in 1946, she painted a large canvas of the Nuremberg war crimes trials for them as well.

The proposed D-Day invasion of Normandy landings (code named Operation Neptune and the largest invasion by sea in history) began on 6 June 1944. It was the prelude to Operation Overlord which would begin the liberation of the German occupied territories in North-West Europe. This highlighted a problem of the numbers of deserters from British forces which loomed large in the summer of 1944. Between that date and 31 March 1945, there were almost 36,400 cases of desertion. Without ration cards or identity cards deserters often turned to crime or looting in order to survive. Although in Germany the penalty for desertion was capital punishment, this did not generally happen in England. Sentences for penal servitude or hard labour were usually handed out instead. Nevertheless, in Britain desertions increased, perhaps encouraged by memories of Dunkerque. However, there was great mobilisation of the Armed Forces at this time. Normanton Barracks near Derby, a depot of the Sherwood Foresters, was busy and eyewitness accounts of Alfreton also reported large numbers of soldiers in the area. Utmost secrecy about the D-Day campaign was necessary in order to take the Germans by surprise and this proved to be very successful. Although the D-Day campaign took longer than had been expected, the operation was a victory for the Allies and the beginning of the end for the Germans.

In July and August, the 1st Derbyshire Yeomanry fought in the advance to Florence and at the Battle of Monte Cassino, while 2nd and 14th battalions of the Sherwood Foresters had taken part in the assault on Anzio in January of 1944. After Rome fell, the 2nd, 5th and 14th battalions continued fighting in Italy until the 5th Battalion was dispatched in December to deal with the Greek Civil War which had broken out in the aftermath of the German withdrawal. The 14th Battalion was subsequently disbanded and its members posted either to the 2nd or 5th Battalion.

On 12 November, the German battleship, *Tirpitz,* a sister ship of the *Bismarck,* was sunk by British Lancaster bombers equipped with 'tallboy bombs' and over 1,000 German sailors were lost. The 'relentless battering of the German war machine', as the *Manchester Guardian* had termed it, had begun. Allied air bombing was now on a massive scale. As confidence in German defeat grew a new 'dim-out' had replaced the 'black-out' in September. This meant that lighting the equivalent of moonlight was now allowed, although a full black-out would be reimposed if the alert sounded. Night-training exercises and the curse of the Peak District aircraft wrecks were still claiming victims. This time it was the turn of Australian Air Force pilots. On 21 January Wellington Mk.III BJ652/Z was flying from RAF Church Broughton to Lichfield via Suffolk and Yorkshire with six Australian Air Force crew members. The weather had remained reasonable for flying and the aircraft was seen approaching Baslow on its homeward stretch. Minutes later the aircraft flew into a rock outcrop near Youlgreave, killing all the crew members and destroying the plane. It was estimated that the plane may have been flying at 2,000ft (610m), a little low but it had begun its landing descent. However, it was pointed out that the change in air pressure during the course of the flight could have caused the altimeter to give faulty readings, by as much as 90ft (27.5m), which meant that the pilot would have believed the plane was flying at a higher altitude than it really was. A few weeks later, in mid-March, Oxford Mk.I LX745/B was also flying on a night exercise with a crew of three. Visibility was poor and wind speeds were fluctuating and radio calls from the aircraft do not seem to have been answered. The aircraft was found on Shining Tor near Buxton after being missing for five days. Clearly disorientated, the pilot had flown too low, hitting the ground with a wing and had then flown through a wall causing the aircraft to disintegrate. There were no survivors. Just a couple of weeks later, again on night-flight exercises, Armstrong Whitworth Albemarle G.T. Mk.I P1463 came to grief near Ashbourne. It was a night of snow showers and poor visibility and the plane finally took off three hours late. However, a minute or so after take-off the aircraft hit high-tension cables which caused it to 'slew to port', hit the top of a tree, then flew down a nearby valley before appearing to crash-land. All four crew were killed and the subsequent Court of Inquiry blamed ice on the wings and tail as an important contributory factor in the crash. Shining Tor would claim another victim in November. North American Harvard Mk.IIB FT442 was on a solo training flight with a young Czechoslovakian pilot at the controls. He was returning to base in thick cloud and simply flew in to the ground on the eastern slope of Shining Tor and was killed outright. On Midsummer Day the moors above Howden claimed another victim. Stirling Mk.III LJ628 crashed into the hillside of Upper Commons on Howden Moor after flying into heavy cloud. All nine people aboard survived and only two had injuries. It was one of the luckier outcomes of the Dark Peak wrecks. Shining Tor near Buxton also claimed another victim on 24 September. Noorduyn UC-64A Norseman 43-35439 belonging to the USAAF was being flown from Burtonwood to Newark and back. On the return journey there was low cloud over the hills and a strong headwind. When the pilot judged he was clear of the hills he began his descent. He was not clear and the aircraft struck the ground, flipped over and caught fire. The pilot managed to escape although thoroughly shaken up and in shock. In October it was the turn of Glossop to experience a Peak District aircraft wreck. On 11 October B-J24 Liberator 42-52003 was being flown from Burtonwood to Hardwick. The altimeter indicated they were 2,800ft (853.5m) above the ground but they were in heavy cloud and experiencing severe turbulence. Through a gap in the clouds the pilot suddenly realised that they were only 150ft (46m) above the ground and immediately tried to gain height, but too little too late. The aircraft struck the ground on Mill Hill between Hayfield and Glossop. Although injured the two crew members managed to get out of the cockpit and walked until they found the Glossop road where they were picked up by a passing vehicle. Both were treated for minor injuries and both knew that they had had a very lucky escape. At the beginning of November Oxford Mk.I HN429 was on a training flight from Cheshire with a crew of three aboard. The trainee pilot lost his way over the unfamiliar territory and the plane struck the northern side of Axe Edge near Buxton. All three crew survived, although with injuries, and the student pilot had to have his right foot amputated. Two weeks before Christmas Kinder Scout had claimed yet another crash. Avro Anson Mk.I N9853 was flying Polish staff from Nottinghamshire to RAF Millom. There was thick cloud over Kinder, as is so often the case, causing disorientation and the aircraft struck the ground on Edale Moor and overturned. Incredibly, all five men on board escaped with mostly minor injuries and were treated at the RAF hospital in Wilmslow.

Food, both quality and quantity, was still high on the agenda. The government had decided that the quality of strawberry and raspberry jam needed to be improved. In addition, apricot pulp had been purchased and brought in from Spain to make apricot jam. The 'wonders of dehydration' were discussed by Parliament. What this basically meant was the drying of vegetables which could be reconstituted as needed but would take up much less storage and carriage. The Minister of Food quoted the case of 1,000 tons of cabbage dried and reduced to 40 tons. He then went on to enthusiastically describe a new product:

> ...mashed potato powder, which was contained in a tin much like cocoa powder...one took a few teaspoons, poured hot water on it and got a very good mashed potato without any cooking in the home...I do not think anyone would know that it was not ordinary mashed potato.

To the generation which grew up on 'Smash' this statement might raise a few wry smiles. However, dried foods lose some of their nutritional value in the dehydration process and this fact had to be considered against possible savings in tonnage. The troops needed every bit of energy they could muster from rations which were not overly generous; and hard-working traditional Derbyshire farmers, who grew their own potatoes anyway, were not going to eat a powdered replacement which had none of the bite or fibre of home-cooked potatoes.

The summer of 1944 brought a fresh menace from the skies. This was the V-1 rocket, the 'buzz bomb' or 'doodlebug' as it was nicknamed because of the buzzing sound that was one of its chief characteristics. It was a monoplane which had no pilot. The fuselage was manufactured from welded sheet steel and the wings were made of plywood; and its 'Argus-built pulse-jet engine pulsed 50 times per second' which is what produced the dreaded buzzing sound. The V-1 was either ground launched, using an aircraft catapult, or air launched from a bomber plane. It was unable to take off independently due to the low engine thrust and problems with the small wings. Code-named 'Cherry Stone', the 'V' stood for Vengeance weapon (Vergeltungswaffen) but it initially had a limited range (150 miles or 240km) and most were fired at London or on Southern England. The missile was pre-set to trigger the arming of its warhead after about 37 miles (60km) and when the detonating bolts were fired the V-1 went into a steep dive which caused the engine to stop. The sudden silence alerted those below that impact was imminent. A boy in Buxton described his terror when he first heard the noise of a doodlebug and the even more terrifying moments of silence. Another lad in Clowne (not far from Sheffield) saw a doodlebug pass over on its way, he believed, to the steel works in Sheffield, but it crashed harmlessly on moorland some way short of its target. Derbyshire was fortunate in a way in that the Germans didn't specifically aim the flying bombs at the county. They were more interested in taking out industry, railway lines and manufacturing complexes, so they aimed for the towns and cities; especially southern towns and cities, but also places like Manchester, Stockport, Leeds, Sheffield, and Liverpool. The main problem was that the doodlebugs or buzz bombs were not always very accurate in their aim. The Luftwaffe were also using Heinkel He 111 bombers to cross the North Sea and launch V-1 bombs, or doodlebugs, as well, so that the V-1 bombs now had a greater range. Between 100–150 flying bombs were being fired each day. Doodlebugs hit their targets about half an hour after launching. Remembering the Christmas blitz on cities in 1940 and dreading a renewal, the people of Derbyshire were not particularly confident that they would be spared from fresh bomb attacks, although bomb damage in the county had been modest by comparison with places like Manchester or Coventry. They were right to be concerned, as early in the morning of Christmas Eve 1944, almost four years to the day after the Christmas blitz of 1940, the Germans launched a total of forty-five V-1s against Manchester. However, fourteen fell in the North Sea so that only thirty-one made it across the Channel into Yorkshire. Of these just seven reached the area now known as Greater Manchester and one which fell on a field of sprouts at Didsbury was the single successful hit in the city and suburbs of Manchester. Six fell on towns like Stockport and Radcliffe in what is now Greater Manchester, but the one which caused the most damage landed instead on Tottington, a small Lancashire town between Bury and Ramsbottom. The bomb which hit Stockport fell on Garners Lane. Two houses were destroyed, several others damaged, and a car was burned out; but amazingly only one person was killed, although there were some seriously injured casualties. The remaining twenty-four doodlebug bombs intended for the city landed in the surrounding counties of Cheshire, Derbyshire and Yorkshire. Buildings up to a mile from the crash sites were damaged, but there was no widespread destruction and comparatively few fatalities.

Hopes had faded that the war would be over by Christmas 1944, but the tide of the war had turned and there were new initiatives on both the battle fronts and home front. The YMCA had instigated a scheme whereby they would deliver Christmas gifts to the relatives of those serving abroad. The father of one family paid for a Christmas tree to be delivered to his family while he was serving in Italy. The British War Relief Society (BWRS) also paid for Christmas cards, savings stamps and gifts for children this Christmas. The BRWS coordinated charities in the United States which had raised funding to provide the British with clothes, food and non-military aid. The black-out was reduced as the threat from German bombers was now practically non-existent, and churches were allowed to light up their windows for Christmas. The Ministry of Food allowed extra meat, sugar and sweet rations as a Yuletide treat. However, on Christmas Eve, a fleet of thirty doodlebugs attacked the northern part of the country from Derby to Durham. It was a sharp reminder that the war was not quite over yet.

CHAPTER SEVEN

1945

By 1945 the 2nd Battalion of the Sherwood Foresters was in Palestine and the 5th Battalion had returned to Italy from Greece. They then marched on Austria with the liberation armies. Both battalions had acquitted themselves well, earning seven battle honours in North Africa and a further eleven battle honours in Italy. Meanwhile, the 1st Derbyshire Yeomanry were fighting in Italy in April 1945, and the 2nd Derbyshire Yeomanry won honours fighting on the Lower Maas and then again fighting at Ourthe in the Battle of the Bulge; while the whole regiment also won battle honours 'fighting in the Rhineland and the Reichswald in February and in March for crossing the Rhine during Operation Plunder'. The bombing of Dresden by the RAF and the USAAF took place between 13–15 February. It was a savage and prolonged attack which, ultimately, was in revenge for the vicious ravages of the Blitz, and a kind of turning point. The RAF sent 722 heavy bombers together with 527 from the USAF and dropped nearly 4,000 tons of high explosive bombs and incendiary bombs on the city. This created a firestorm which destroyed the city centre and an estimated 25,000 lives were lost. Derbyshire folk, remembering the inferno of the Blitz created by the Germans, not to mention the terrible mess made of cities like London, Liverpool, Manchester and Coventry by the Blitz, felt that the Germans were now getting a long overdue taste of their own medicine, but there were a number of citizens who shuddered at the huge loss of civilian lives, especially those of children. They recalled only too well how it felt to lose members of their own families. At the same time, they understood that it was the German military machine which had caused their sufferings, not the civilians of German cities, and they sympathised to some extent with how it felt to be bombed without mercy. Two further USAAF raids on Dresden followed which were aimed at destroying the city's railway yard and there was yet another one in April on the neighbouring industrial areas. In the seventy plus years since the bombing of Dresden claim and counter claim have been furiously argued. Was it necessary? Was it over-reaction? Was it just German propaganda which made it seem so appalling? Was it an 'innocent city of culture' or a centre of munitions and armament manufacturing? Was it simply an attempt to scare the Germans into surrender? It was all and none of these things. To read accounts of the bombing of Dresden is dreadful. To read accounts of the Blitz on English cities is dreadful.

It might have been the last year of the war but the toll of aircraft wrecks in the Peak District continued to rise. On 21 January USAAF aircraft, C-47 Dakota 42-93683, should have been nowhere near this area. The brief of this daytime training flight was to fly a circular route from Chalgrove in Oxfordshire to Wrexham on the Welsh border to Bury St Edmunds in Suffolk and back to Chalgrove. However, bad weather was closing in and, after Wrexham, the plane changed its flight path to a more northerly route. After a while the crew lost visibility of the ground altogether. Worried, the pilot started to climb to gain some height, but hit the tops of trees almost immediately which forced a crash-landing of the plane somewhere between Buxton and Ashbourne. The crew were unhurt but there was some cosmetic damage to the aircraft. The aircraft was just another victim of the treacherous conditions and weather which often surround the Peak District and the outcome was much more fortunate than it could have been, especially in the middle of winter. A month later three planes crashed in the same area on the same day at Tintwistle Knarr in the Longdendale Valley close to Glossop. On 22 February three Hawker Hurricanes, PZ851, PZ765, and PZ854 took off from Nantwich to practise formation flying and they were instructed to avoid cloud cover. This they did but they could not avoid the industrial smog haze of Manchester which blurred visibility (and still does although the main modern cause is traffic rather than manufactories). Although the Longdendale Valley is a few miles out from Manchester the 'smog haze' still drifts over it today, and in 1945 it was likely to have been much thicker. Unable to see the ground clearly the three planes simply flew into the hillside of Tintwistle Knarr. Each aircraft shattered on impact and burst into flames, killing each of the three pilots. Two weeks later poor visibility over the hills again claimed two more crash victims. The first, Airspeed Oxford Mk.I NM683, was on a cross-country map-reading exercise. It had taken off from RAF Warboys in Cambridgeshire and was heading for Warrington. There was cloud cover on the hills, but a decision was made that it would be safe to fly beneath it. As the aircraft descended it flew straight into the ground at Rushup Edge near Edale. Amazingly, although the plane was wrecked, none of the four crew were seriously injured. The following day Percival Proctor Mk.III HM324 was not so lucky. Again in low cloud, the aircraft flew into a hillside near Buxton, the plane was wrecked but this time all three crew were killed. Before the war was finally over Bleaklow claimed two more victims and the moors above Glossop also claimed another victim. On 18 May, Lancaster Mk.X KB 993 was on a training flight from RAF Linton-on-Ouse but became disorientated as darkness fell. Just after 10 pm the aircraft was seen by witnesses to fly into the ground at James' Thorn close to Higher Shelf Stones on Bleaklow. All six crew on board were killed. Eleven days later a USAAF plane, North American P-51D Mustang 44-64084, crashed near Glossop on a flight from Debden to Speke. Low cloud had disorientated the pilot and the aircraft crashed into the ground at high speed causing a sizeable crater. The pilot was killed instantly. The final wartime aircraft casualty in the Derbyshire peaks was on 24 July and, again, on Bleaklow. C47-A Dakota 42-108982 was flying from Poix near Amiens to Renfrew, it had landed briefly at Leicester but never arrived at Renfrew: two days later walkers discovered the crash site on Bleaklow. The aircraft had flown into the hillside and was wrecked, and the crew of seven were dead. Once again low cloud was believed to be the culprit.

For those who would like more information on the aircraft wrecks, www.peakdistrictaircrashes.co.uk is an excellent website on which much of the information about the Peak District air crash sites is written and recorded by Alan Clark. Another excellent source is *Dark Peak Aircraft Wrecks vol.1* (Ron Collier and Ronnie Wilkinson; first published 1982). It is important to remember that little remains of most wrecks, many of which are in locations that are remote and difficult to access. A few are on private land and permission should always be requested from the landowner by anyone who would like to visit such a site. Little of the actual aircraft involved in the crashes has been left in situ but, where this is the case, please do not take souvenirs. A plane crash site, like those of shipwrecks, officially designated is a memorial site. Sometimes relatives of those who died in the aircraft crashes have erected small memorials to those they have lost. Please respect them. There have been a number of cases of vandalism or destruction of such memorials at Derbyshire wartime sites and that is an insensitive insult to the dead as well as a criminal offence.

Bleaklow Moors, site of several plane crashes during the 1940s.

In mid-March, almost two months before the European war ended, the government had realised that further call-up of military personnel would be required for the war against Japan. The army was now well equipped and well trained but new manpower would need time to be fully trained and assimilated. Besides which it was recognised that the process of redeployment against Japan would be a complicated and difficult process. Japan's aim of bombing Pearl Harbour in 1941 was to acquire much needed extra territory for its population and the raw materials of rubber, tin and oil. They had also gained Hong Kong and Indo-China as well as the Malay peninsula, Singapore and the Dutch East Indies, before embarking on the infamous Burma campaign. This would give them overland access to China and enable them to cut off supplies to the army of Chiang Kai-shek; and it would also leave them well placed to reach Assam and fan the flames of insurrection against the British Raj in India. The Japanese were fierce fighters and Allied troops found themselves up against an enemy who was very determined, aggressive, and pretty merciless towards prisoners of war, as well as the natural enemies of snakes, scorpions, mosquitos and crocodiles.

Hitler committed suicide on 30 April and the treaty of surrender was signed by the Germans a week later. V-E Day or Victory in Europe Day was celebrated on 7 May by the Commonwealth countries; on 8 May in Britain and Europe; and on 9 May in the Channel Islands. Derbyshire welcomed peace with a huge sigh of relief and many impromptu parties. There was sheer joy and exuberance that Germany was defeated, Hitler was dead, and peacetime had come again. Lights shone once more in windows everywhere, Victory bonfires blazed, and the church bells rang out, but the war was not completely over, however. The Allies were still at war with Japan and the Japanese government refused to surrender to the Allied Forces despite the Allied call for total Japanese surrender at the Potsdam Conference on 27 July. Invasion was considered but finally rejected in favour of using the so far untested atomic bomb. On 6 August the first atomic bomb was dropped on Hiroshima killing 66,000 of its 255,000 citizens and injuring another 69,000, according to American figures. The Japanese still refused to surrender so Russia declared war on Japan and invaded Manchuria on 8 August, but the US had lost patience. The following day Nagasaki was bombed. Out of a population of 195,000 there were 39,000 dead and 25,000 injured, again according to US figures. Absolute figures are difficult to assess, as atomic explosions create firestorms which can cover several miles incinerating everything in their path, and radiation sickness can kill many years after the event. By this time there was a division between the Japanese military who wanted to continue the fight and Japanese civilians who simply wanted an end to the nightmare bombing and to live in peace. The Japanese Emperor, Hirohito, whom many Japanese regarded as divine, had never really been in favour of the war but he had had little choice except to go along with it. After the bombing of Nagasaki it was Emperor Hirohito who finally insisted that the war should end. Five days later Japan surrendered to the Allies and 14 August was designated V-J (Victory in Japan) day.

Derbyshire marked V-J Day, but it was not with quite the same rush of initial enthusiasm with which V-E Day had been greeted, although Derbyshire men were involved as the 1/5th Battalion of the Sherwood Foresters had been sent to Singapore in 1942, arriving shortly before it fell to the Japanese. Subsequently, they were captured by the Japanese and made to work on the Burma-Siam railway. Despite the cruelty of the Japanese towards their prisoners, the Burma Campaign was hailed as the forgotten war and the fight against the Japanese in South East Asia largely forgotten except by those who had the misfortune to endure it. None of the survivors ever really recovered from the brutalities they suffered. The building of the bridge over the River Kwai by Allied forces was probably a better-known incident than the war itself. Nevertheless, despite the personal tragedies, Derbyshire could now tell itself that it had survived another World War with honour.

Although demobilisation of troops would start soon, other wartime conditions would continue, and chief among these was rationing. Rationing would remain for some years and even increased in the case of certain commodities. To the astonishment of Derbyshire folk, allowances of meat, bacon, cooking fat and soap were further reduced only two weeks after V-E Day. Derbyshire was further amazed when, despite the war being over, bread was finally rationed. It had not been rationed during the war and people had raised their hopes of being able to eat white bread once more. Anyone who had hoped for, or could afford, a break after the war had ended found that the railways were sadly depleted. During the war freight and military requirements had been primary factors, rolling stock was ageing and a considerable amount of it had been damaged by enemy action. Train services were curtailed and running times were uncertain. The time of austerity was certainly far from over. However, on 16 June the Family Allowances Act was passed awarding mothers a tax-free cash payment for each child. It was the first time in Britain that a payment from the State had been given directly to women.

As the war ended the National Union of Agricultural Workers set up a Derby branch and discovered an unusual problem. The Land Army was due to be dissolved and farmers would lose a lot of comparatively cheap and very efficient labour. Parallel to this event was the problem of PoW labour. PoWs were cheap to employ, and there was a fear that when the regular farm workers returned from the war they would find that their jobs had been taken by cheaper labour. The unions were equally concerned. In Derby there was quite a large Italian community as a result of the internment of all Italian males in 1940. They had worked as farm labourers, builders' assistants, quarry hands, and in the railway workshops, living in various PoW camps within the county. There was also a downturn in the economy due to the frenzied production of items for the war effort being no longer necessary. There were redundancies and employers began to hope for a return to the 'free market' where, as they saw it, their hands would not be tied at every turn. Union membership began to decline and there was some competition for amalgamation to maintain numbers and influence. Wage agreements were becoming national rather than local. Derby was a definite centre for union activity and there were a large number of different unions, some with impossibly long tongue-twisters of names. They all had a common aim: that of benefitting their members and ensuring that the employment market did not return to the harsh days of Cottonopolis, although each treasured their own individuality. Towns like Chesterfield, Glossop, Buxton, and Ashbourne, all had different unions who were active in various industries, but the National Union of Agricultural Workers was prevalent in the countryside. Derbyshire was quite an aware and politically motivated county. Most unions had increased their membership during the war years, peaking in 1945, and had been successful in improving wages and working conditions for their members. This came at a price, however. Average wages rose by 63 per cent during the war years while prices only increased by under 4 per cent. This indicated that wages had been woefully inadequate before the war, but profits had been greatly reduced which did not please either business owners or the shareholders.

There was also a further shock in store for the citizens of Britain. The liberating armies of the Allied forces in Germany and Poland had stumbled across possibly the most appalling war crime of all time. Soldiers were unable to believe the sights which greeted them when they reached concentration camps like Auschwitz and Bergen-Belsen. There were dozens of such camps across Germany and Poland but these two had acquired a reputation for unrivalled savagery towards their inmates. People, little more than bags of bones in the infamous blue-and-white striped utility clothing used by these establishments, clung to barriers in an effort to stand upright. Equally they could not believe the sight of the liberating forces. Their Nazi gaolers had been brutal to the last. The 'lucky ones', if they could be called that, were at least still alive. They had survived the brutality, the beatings, the abuse, the rapes and the medical experiments, but at a terrible personal cost. Allied soldiers had tears in their eyes as they gazed at these skeletal scraps of humanity clinging to the wire fences and gave them whatever provisions they could. The full horror of what had happened emerged slowly from piecing together the prisoners' stories, interrogating captured Nazi guards, and discovering at least some of the records which the Germans had tried to destroy. Day after day trains had arrived at these camps with their human cargo loaded into cattle trucks. The trucks were unloaded, the inmates rapidly sorted into groups. After the briefest of examinations, any pretty girls, musicians and exceptionally fit looking young men were selected for survival but it was only comparative few who were spared. The rest were then dispatched to the reception huts. Here they were ordered to undress completely and to remove any personal effects. Told that they were going to have showers before the distribution of clothing and personal effects, they were then herded like cattle towards the buildings where their lives would be ended prematurely in complete and utter degradation. Packed into huge chambers, the doors were then slammed shut and locked. Keen to preserve illusions until the last to prevent panic and opposition, the chambers had the appearance of massive showers. However, it was not water which was pumped into the chambers but a lethal toxic gas which choked, burned and asphyxiated victims. Men, women and children died together. Over 6 million Jews were killed, exterminated like vermin in the huge gas chambers, as part of Hitler's 'final solution'. The people of Derbyshire like everyone else, were horrified, but some of them had Jewish children as evacuees. How could they ever even begin to explain to them? How could this be allowed to happen? Who knew? Were all Germans intrinsically evil? The answer was simply that many Germans didn't know anything about the camps until after the war was over, and when they did, most were as shocked as anyone else. Hitler, the SS and the Nazi High Command had insisted on absolute secrecy over such matters and they had complete control of the news outlets. They did not want these activities known and anyone who raised questions often just disappeared. Hitler had been anxious to promote a vision of the good life under the Nazis, hence his insistence on the 'model occupation' of the Channel Islands and now, along with everyone else, Channel Island evacuees would also learn the terrible truth.

The Commonwealth War Graves Commission was originally founded in 1917 by Fabian Ware with the aim of commemorating all those who died in the service of their country in the Great War, and subsequently, the Second World War, by name on a memorial or on a uniform grave headstone (to avoid class distinction) although the actual body of the serviceman might be missing from the grave. The commemoration of those who died in the Great War had tended more towards war memorials of some description. However, by the time of the Second World War many town and village graveyards had begun to include these Commonwealth War Grave headstones in their burial grounds. The grave itself might sometimes be empty but commemoration had been provided in the same manner as for people who did not die as a result of the war. This was especially important for aircraft personnel who died in locations far from home when their plane crashed, or was shot down, or a parachute jump failed. In France and Belgium there are hundreds of tiny cemeteries, some in the middle of fields far from any village, which were the sites of fiercely fought land battles and soldiers lay where they fell. Britain was never occupied, so many of the casualties were from aerial fighting and included British, Polish, Canadian, Australian, American, some French and even a few German individuals. Numerous bodies of servicemen were repatriated after the war, but equally many were never found, especially those who had died in naval battles or bombings. Some churches grouped their Commonwealth graves together in

Commonwealth War Grave in Padfield cemetery, near Glossop, of a victim of one of the many Derbyshire plane crashes in the Second World War.

a secluded corner of the graveyard (as at Bakewell); some placed them in prominent neat rows (as in Buxton cemetery, Ashbourne Cemetery, or Derby [Nottingham Road] cemetery); while others integrated and interspersed them with burials of local people (as in Glossop cemetery, Belper graveyard, or Chesterfield Spital Cemetery). The neat, rectangular headstones, made from pale Portland stone or Hopton Wood stone, are of even height, evenly placed, and easy to recognise. Each headstone displays a cross, unless the person it commemorates is not of the Christian faith, or of any faith at all, and either an emblem of their country or a badge of the regiment in which they served. The stone also shows the name, age, military rank, unit and date of death for that person. There are Commonwealth war graves and dedicated Commonwealth graveyards in a number of countries. In Britain, where there are Commonwealth war graves in a town or village graveyard, there is a plaque on the churchyard gate simply stating 'Commonwealth War Graves'. The sheer numbers of these graves begins to give some idea of the scale of human losses in the Second World War. It also gives grieving loved ones somewhere to go where they can remember and feel close to those they have lost.

In Derbyshire, as everywhere else, those who had survived the war united with those who had lost loved ones in the hope that this really was an end to all wars. History so far (2018) has avoided another world war but there are numbers of bloody skirmishes in many countries and it seems that the prophecy of the ancient Greek historian, Thucydides, that history is cyclical, is likely to prove true and that the human propensity for attack, aggression and domination will remain undimmed.

Row of Commonwealth war graves in Buxton cemetery.

Epilogue

Unexpectedly rationing hadn't stopped with victory for the Allies. Rationing would remain in force for some years and even increased in the case of certain commodities. Sweets were the last commodity to be derationed and that did not happen until 1953, eight years after peace had been declared. For foods that weren't rationed the points system still remained. Each person had 24 points to last them for four weeks. Points were in addition to money paid for the goods but it meant, for example, that no one could buy more than two large bars of toilet soap per month. This was aimed not only at rationing but also to deter hoarding and profiteering. Some foods cost large numbers of points; others were not so bad. A pound (just under 500kg) of rice required 8 points; a tin of baked beans 2 points; a pound (just under 500g) of currants needed 16 points while a tin of sardines only took 2 points. Folk still had to plan carefully and needed to remember their ration books and their points allowances if they were away from home. Everyone was allowed 4 soap coupons for four weeks. A large tablet of toilet soap cost 2 coupons. Clothing coupons were also scarce. Each person was allowed clothing coupons which might have to last up to a year. It was not an overly generous allowance. A man's overcoat required 16 coupons; a suit would cost 26 coupons; a pair of trousers needed 8 coupons and a pair of underpants 4 coupons. The ladies fared little better: a dress needed 7 coupons; a nightdress 6 points; a mackintosh 16 points; and knickers were 3 points a pair. Making the coupons last, or affording special clothes like a wedding dress, became a great skill. Make do and mend was still very much the order of the day. Coal, coke and paraffin supplies were also limited.

There was great excitement about the post-war election to be held on 5 July 1945. There had been a coalition government throughout the war and Churchill had received the necessary support from its Labour members. Labour Party members had pulled their weight on the home front. Soldiers, sailors and airmen who held Labour beliefs had fought hard for their country. Labour Party members and believers in socialist principles had given their all to defeat fascism every bit as much as Conservative members and believers.

Britain had been hailed as the most mobilised country in the war. Its female population had thrown themselves into the war effort, ably supporting and assisting the male population. This was supposedly the secret of its success and eventual victory. Furthermore, there had been no mention by the Conservatives of implementing anything contained in the Beveridge Report. Clement Attlee, the leader of the Labour Party, seized the moment, and he was quite unequivocal in his proposals for the future. Labour's manifesto (entitled 'Let Us Face the Future') contained proposals to nationalise the Bank of England, fuel and power, inland transport and iron and steel. Government intervention would be necessary, the party argued, to keep a check on raw materials, food prices and employment. Following the Beveridge Report of 1942, the Labour Party also formed plans to create a National Health Service and social security (BBC *The People's War*). Churchill, however, came out strongly against the Labour Party and its socialist aims and principles:

> *I must tell you that a socialist policy is abhorrent to British ideas on freedom... a socialist state could not afford to suffer opposition - no socialist system can be established without a political police... [a Labour government] would have to fall back on some form of Gestapo...*

> *(Winston Churchill 1945)*

It was an extremely unfortunate choice of words linking a Labour government to the Gestapo and, unsurprisingly, Labour won a landslide victory with an overall majority of 146. Churchill was shocked, and he felt completely betrayed. He could not believe that he had led the British people successfully through the biggest war in history only to have them turn their backs on him. The facts were a little more prosaic. Churchill was an excellent wartime leader. That was his time. He was not a peacetime leader. His bulldog attitude, his impatience and his often harsh dismissal of issues and ideas, especially those concerning the working classes, were not suited to the changing society which was evolving after the war. This was Clement Attlee's time.

Shortly after the defeat of Germany in 1945 William Joyce was arrested near the Danish border and subsequently tried for treason. He was executed on that charge at HMP Wandsworth in January 1946, still defiant, still blaming the Jews for the Second World War and 'the darkness which the Jews represent' but ranting against a new enemy which he now perceived to be communism and the Soviet Union. There were protests that Britain had no right to do this as Joyce was both an Irish and an American citizen and so therefore officially under their protection. However, Joyce also held a British passport, and the prosecution successfully claimed that by doing this he was, at the time, technically a British citizen. His wife, Margaret, initially held as a military prisoner in Holloway, was spared, for the unconvincing reason that 'she had suffered enough.' She was deported to Germany where she was

War memorial, Earl Sterndale.

interned, although she eventually returned to Britain, where she died, largely unmourned, in the 1970s.

Evacuees returned to their homes, some reluctantly, many of them with fond memories and having made friends for life. Most of their hosts were sad to see them go and kept in touch. In 1990 some of the children who had been evacuated from Lowestoft made a nostalgic return trip to Glossop, the town that had opened its doors and its hearts to them, meeting the daughter of the billeting officer who had allocated their 'foster' homes to them. For evacuees, reuniting with their families could sometimes be difficult. One young lad, encouraged to read as much as he could by the Derbyshire 'foster mother' with whom he had been billeted, was given a number of books to take with him when he returned home. His own mother was intensely disapproving, and every time she saw him reading she told him to stop wasting his time and to do some 'real' work. Over sixty years after the war had ended, All Saints Church in Sudbury installed four memorial glass windows to evacuees which were paid for by former child evacuees from the inner-city suburbs of Manchester who had been fostered in Sudbury. The windows were in two pairs, the top one of each pair showing the dove of peace. One bottom window showed a little girl with her suitcase and bore the caption 'I was a stranger' and its facing pair showed a schoolboy clutching his gas mask and a paper bag with the caption 'and you took me in.'

After the war the Harpur Hill site near Buxton became one of the centres for the destruction of chemical weapons. Nevertheless, after the RAF finally left the site in 1960 the tunnels were used as a mushroom farm. Subsequently they were used as a cold store for cheese, and there was also a warehouse for bonded wines and spirits. Derby University built a campus in the middle of

HSE site and tunnels Harpur Hill, Buxton.

Harpur Hill village for the High Peak area, although this college is no longer in use (2018). The tunnels are still in use today, but there is no public access to them. The site is extensive and has the appearance of multiple hummocks, broad raised banks and several hollows, all of which are of considerable size; some with structures on top. Padlocked double doors in the hillsides indicate entrances to some of the tunnels and underground resources; and it has been labelled Britain's 'Area 51'. Currently the Health and Safety Executive have several laboratories there and the tunnels are used for various purposes. There is also a kind of 'graveyard' for Jubilee Line underground trains, some of which, in the aftermath of the London bombings of the early twenty-first century, have been used to assess the effects of explosions in confined spaces. However, the disused railway line through the site has been closed to walkers so the trains are not accessible to the public. Much of the site is protected by sturdy wooden or barbed wire fencing and security is very strict. Although many surrounding public footpaths are marked on Ordnance Survey maps, some are closed, and others are contentious; so those who visit Harpur Hill (the hill with the tunnels, not the village of the same name nearby) are strongly advised to keep to the public tarmac roads across the area. Quarrying activity still continues on Harpur Hill today, and there is also an adjacent industrial estate which mainly houses scrapyards and vehicle haulage sites. Far Hill Quarry is now disused and flooded and has proved to be very popular with local swimmers because of the beautiful tropical blue hue of the water, which has led to it being known locally as the Blue Lagoon. However, due to the toxicity of chemicals in the surrounding rocks, the lagoon has a pH factor of 11.3 which is what gives the water its attractive colour. To put this in perspective, the optimum safe pH factor for a chlorinated swimming pool is 7.4 because this is the same as the pH level in human eyes. Bleach has a pH factor of 12.6 so the Blue Lagoon water is approaching the level of bleach which is extremely harmful to swimmers.

One of the strangest legacies of the Second World War for Derbyshire has been the sighting of so-called 'ghost planes', especially over Bleaklow and Howden Moor in the Dark Peak, in the Derwent Valley around the Ladybower Reservoir, and in the Longdendale Valley on the Derbyshire-Yorkshire border above Woodhead. The planes are often described as Lancaster bombers and they are usually seen close to where one of the numerous military plane crashes took place. The High Peak still has the unenviable reputation of being a graveyard for Second World War planes. Matters finally came to a head in March 1997 when a number of people in different locations within the area of the Longdendale Valley rang police to report a low flying aircraft, a loud explosion and an orange glow in the sky. The large number of reports, including one from a police patrol car, convinced the police that a major incident had occurred and they called in the emergency services, helicopters, local mountain rescue teams, and tracker dogs. The moors were searched meticulously but no trace of any aircraft was found and there were no reports of any aircraft missing. After twenty-four hours the search was called off and officially the incident has remained a total mystery. However, there are a number of possible explanations. There is still military activity in the area and low flying training exercises regularly take place over the moorlands precisely because of their lack of habitation. From the very nature of this activity, information about aircraft and exercises is going to be scant at best. Although planes are now forbidden to break the sound barrier (i.e. fly faster than the speed of sound) over land, some of them do, and this causes a loud boom, similar to an explosion. This was a common occurrence over Suffolk airfields in the 1950s. Some of these booms were accompanied by a flash of light immediately afterwards. Low flying often forms part of military exercises; but also, on some of the remoter parts of the moors above large cities, there are occasionally 'drugs drops'. Most people are used to jet engines these days, but there are still propeller-powered aircraft in regular commercial use, such as the Bombardier used by FlyBe, the Britten-Norman Trislander favoured by Aurigny for their Channel Island flights, or the Twin Otter and Islander planes used to fly from the English mainland to the Isles of Scilly; although it is probably impossible for these propeller driven planes to reach the speed of sound (767mph or 1234kmph). However, sound can reverberate in the hills and it is possible that a lesser sound than that of breaking the sound barrier could be distorted into the noise of a loud explosion. Optical illusions are also common as a result of the angles of uneven terrain. Commercial airliners can seem like lights arising from nowhere and helicopter searchlights can generate reflected light from water or certain types of geology. Nevertheless, up on the dark lonely moors of Derbyshire on a wild and windy night with the moon partly hidden by cloud, rational explanations do not always seem the most appealing or convincing, and the jury is still out on the continued sightings of 'ghost planes'.

On the anniversary of the Dambusters each year, if the weather is reasonable, a Lancaster still flies low along the Upper Derwent Valley and between the towers of the Howden and Derwent reservoirs to commemorate Guy Gibson and his 617 Squadron. Sadly, on the landmark seventy-fifth anniversary in 2018 the winds were too strong for the old Lancaster to make its customary flight. Better that though than it should end up as one of the Peak District aircraft victims. The Ladybower Reservoir has been flooded for seventy years now but in a dry season, when the waters are low, remains of the two villages are sometimes visible. Other features from the Second World War, such as pillboxes, bunkers, underground shelters, starfish sites, and the network of RAF airfields have largely disappeared. The evacuation of schoolchildren is fast becoming a distant memory as the minimum age of those evacuated is now approaching 80; and it is the museums, oral history archives, film studies, history books, war memorials, and Commonwealth graves which are now keeping the remembrances of the Second World War alive for Derbyshire as for everywhere else.

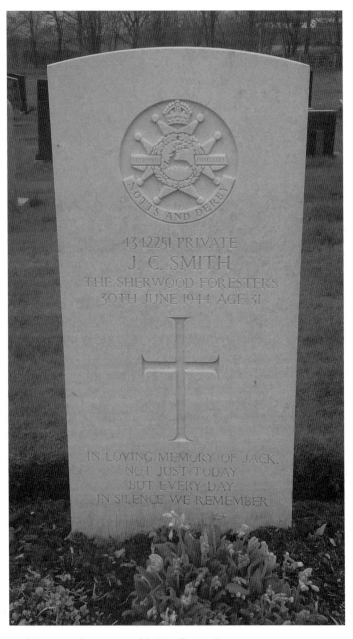

Sherwood Forester Commonwealth War Grave, Buxton.

Part of Stoney Middleton quarry works.

Bibliography

Books

Collier, Ron, and Wilkinson, Ronnie, *Dark Peak Aircraft Wrecks vol.1* (first published 1982)

Hallam, Vic, *Lest We Forget: The Dambusters in the Upper Derwent Valley* (1993)

Hallam, Vic, *Silent Valley: The Story of the Lost Derbyshire Villages of Derwent and Ashopton* (1987)

Mawson, Gillian, *Guernsey Evacuees* (The History Press)

McCamley, Nick, *Disasters Underground*, pp. 48-56

Museums, etc.

Derbyshire Record Office

Derbyshire TGWU records

Glossop Reference library

Imperial War Museum North

Manchester Central Library

National Coal Mining Museum (near Wakefield)

Newspapers

Derby Telegraph

Glossop Chronicle 1939-45

Online Sources

'An Introduction to Starfish, Civil Decoys and Sheffield's Wartime Passive Defences' (Calver, Curbar, and Froggatt History. https://ccflocalhistory.wordpress.com/2016/11/24/the-decoy/)

'A People's History of Derbyshire Part II' (Graham Stevenson. www.grahamstevenson.me.uk)

'Crich Parish' (Margaret Smith. www.crichparish.co.uk)

'New Mills Air Raid 1942' (Steve Lewis. www.stevelewis.me.uk)

'Pastscape: Starfish Bombing Decoy Sites' (Historic England. www.pastscape.org.uk)

'Prisoner of War Camp' (Stoney Middleton Heritage. www.smhccg.org/village-history)

'The Harpur Hill Site: its geology, evolutionary history...' (British Geological Survey Report CR/13/104)

The Long Eaton and Sawley Archive (www.long-eaton.com/wartime.asp)

www.peakdistrictaircrashes.co.uk (Alan Clark)

'WW2 People's War' (BBC. www.bbc.co.uk/history/ww2peopleswar)

Index